HAUNTED
CARROLL COUNTY,
OHIO

HAUNTED
CARROLL COUNTY,
OHIO

JANICE VANHORNE-LANE

HAUNTED
America

Published by Haunted America
A Division of The History Press
Charleston, SC
www.historypress.com

Front cover: A current look at St. Mary's of the Immaculate Conception in Morges, Ohio. *Courtesy Enna Lame Photography.*
Back cover: Photo of the Cox Mansion scanned from an old negative, date unknown. *Courtesy Jay Stoneman and Isaac Brumm.*

First published 2024

Manufactured in the United States

ISBN 9781467158121

Library of Congress Control Number: 2024937574

CONTENTS

ACKNOWLEDGEMENTS

First, I want to thank Dolly Kertes for being insistent I investigate local hauntings and for encouraging me to do this project. Without her prompting, I would likely have never begun collecting these stories.

Second, a big hug and many thanks to DiAnne Buck. Who would have thought that when I sat in your journalism class—let's just say *many* years ago—I would be writing books on history and have the honor of you serving as a proofreader for me. It warms my heart to have you as a friend and mentor. Your help has meant so much to me. THANKS!

Third, I want to thank everyone who shared their stories with me. It is not easy to tell the stories of things that go bump in the night and not feel like you are being judged. I am truly grateful for each and every one of you who was willing to share. Hopefully, I have done your story justice.

The list of those who have given so graciously of their time to help this poor girl dig through archives of varying sorts, find lost records, and even gone so far as to hand deliver an obituary after hours is extensive. I know that if I try to list all of you, I will miss someone. You know who you are, so THANK YOU! Thanks to the Carroll County Genealogical Society, the Carroll County Historical Society, the Malvern Historical Society, the Stark County Library, the Carroll County Map Office, and the *Free Press Standard* for keeping records and photos and doing their best to maintain those records for the future generations. I especially want to thank Jay Stoneman and Isaac Brumm for scanning photos and negatives. Also, a huge shout-out to all the home and business owners who allowed me to traipse through their yards and take photos. There is no way I could have done all of this without all of you.

To the gals at the Carroll County Coffee Company, thanks for keeping me caffeinated and for listening to my rants while putting all the finishing touches on this project.

I would like to specifically thank Dr. Mandal Haas, our local coroner, for taking time out of his busy schedule to review a death from over one hundred years ago with me. To Rick Weals of Carroll County Paranormal Investigators, thank you for all of your advice, for helping me locate information, and for pointing me in the direction of some of the ghosts. Also, thanks to Terri Eichel for your help on understanding the supernatural side a little more than I did when I started.

I thank my family for their patience as I "vanished" into my office for hours on end and their skills as photographers and artists. I love you!

Lastly, to you the reader. Thank you for picking up this book and deciding to read it. You are what makes doing all the research worth it.

Introduction

Welcome

D riving along the rolling hills of Carroll County, you will see many fields, quaint farmhouses, small towns, and friendly people. What you will not see are the tenants of ages past—those who came and never went. Don't believe in ghosts? Neither did I, and I am still not sure that I do, but I am going to share with you the stories and experiences others shared with me and let you decide for yourself.

As a child, my friends and I often played (as I imagine most children do) at having séances, the game stiff-as-a-board-light-as-a-feather, and with Ouija boards and fortune-telling cards. To us, it was harmless fun, and I suspect while we hoped something spooky would happen, secretly we were glad it did not. But what if we were just lucky? Maybe the "spirits" knew better than to appear to children on demand, or maybe we were in the wrong house.

As an adult in my early twenties, I was quick to dismiss things I heard go bump in the night as, "Oh, the cat probably knocked it over," or "It was probably just the wind." Living out in the country, it was easy to come up with a logical explanation for shadows caught moving out of the corner of my eye or an inanimate object appearing to have moved on its own. I mean, books do not just slide off a perfectly flat and level table, right? There had to have been an earthquake or something, right? Surely that kind of thing could happen in Northeastern Ohio. I mean, surely, I am not the only person to experience objects vanishing and suddenly reappearing, right?

By my thirties, I started to wonder if there really was someone there that I could not physically see. When my youngest daughter was born, we were renting a house in Carrollton. I was nursing her and watching television while my husband was at work and my older daughter was at preschool. I was watching a show about ghosts, and a comment was made about how people often fake their experiences. Very clearly, I heard a man laugh at the statement. I turned to look at the corner of the room where the laugh had come from, and of course, I saw nothing. The cat, which had been lying at my feet, had apparently heard it as well, as he sat up and looked in the same direction. My daughter stopped nursing and looked in that direction. I later learned that the owner's father had passed away in the house many years before.

It was in this same house that we would sometimes notice the smell of cigarette smoke in the downstairs bathroom. None of my family smoked, but friends would visit and complain about the smell. We were told that prior to it being a bathroom, it had been a back porch where the owner's dad would stand and smoke since he was not allowed to smoke in the house. Perhaps he is still there enjoying a smoke every now and then.

I have been told that the more I open my mind up to the idea of unseen beings, the more likely I am to encounter them. I am not sure whether that means I am imagining them or if my acceptance has freed them to come out and make their presence more known. Either way, I have had many more encounters since that house and since writing this book.

A more recent incident occurred while I was working at our church, which is about four miles from town. I am the secretary and spend much of my time there alone. One particular day, the pastor was there too. He was sitting in his office, which is adjacent to mine. I was standing in the doorway between our offices talking to the pastor when we both heard the pitter-patter of little feet running down the hallway. We then heard a giggle from what sounded like a little girl. He asked me to go see who had come into the building. I immediately looked in the hall and saw no one. I headed in the direction the child had been running and found no one. Perplexed, I looked out into the parking lot, and there were no cars. No people. And the child was not to be found. It was a nice fall day. Children living nearby would have been in school, and none of the nearby houses had children younger than school age living in them at the time. When I told the pastor there was no one there, he laughed it off and said I must have imagined it—even though he was the one who told me to go see who was there, so I know he heard it too.

Photo of the Presbyterian manse that was taken for another project. Look carefully at the first-floor window, second from the right. *Courtesy N8 Lane.*

The defining moment was while I was working on my book *Safe Houses and the Underground Railroad in East Central Ohio*. We were in Zanesville, Ohio, and my husband was taking photos of old houses for me with our digital camera. One of the houses was an old Presbyterian Church manse that sits beside the church. We knocked on the door, and there was no answer. I peeked in the windows and saw that there was no furniture in the house, so I assumed it was likely the building was between tenants. It sits on a quiet street away from any major traffic. We crossed the street, and he took a succession of photos. Later, while going through the photos to decide which one would be used for publication, he noticed something in the third photo. He zoomed in, and instantly the hairs on his arm stood up. Clearly staring back at us was a middle-aged Black woman with her head covered with what looked like a do-rag and stirring a big bowl of something. The first two photos showed nothing, and neither did the last two. Only the middle photo. If he had not taken the photos himself, we would have suspected someone had Photoshopped her in. Some would argue that it was a fluke. Fluke or not, these personal encounters have certainly made me a lot less skeptical.

This was the third photo of five in the series taken that day. This is zoomed in to see the image. Reflection or ghost? *Courtesy N8 Lane.*

Do I have answers as to what really happened? No. Nor do I have the ability or resources to explain each and every encounter. I did elicit the help of paranormal investigators, a medium, and the local coroner. As I shared my stories, others stepped forward with their own. So, whether you believe or not, I hope you will enjoy reading about the encounters of others as they were told to me and be entertained either way. And while I did not have fancy equipment and did not go on any ghost hunts or stakeouts or anything, I simply took the time to listen to the stories of those who met their unseen visitors and record them. Many of these locations are genuine and documented haunts, but others may be legends or hearsay. Ghosts and haunts are something we likely will not be able to confirm until we ourselves are one. For now…

Enjoy!

CHAPTER 1

RAPPINGS, KNOCKINGS, AND TAPS

Bah humbug! We have all heard this said by many a man portraying the character of Ebenezer Scrooge. But do you know what the phrase meant back when Charles Dickens wrote it? Beginning in 1751 as a slang term, it was used as an exclamation to describe something as hypocritical nonsense or gibberish. Like many English words that change over time, *humbug* was the word used instead of *ghost* by the 1840s. Humbuggers were folks who believed in ghosts. *Bah* was a sound like someone in the twenty-first century making a noise of disgust. So, "Bah humbug" was simply Mr. Scrooge dismissing the existence of ghosts or saying that it was all gibberish. Reading through the newspapers of the 1850s, you may see the word quite often. Most of the time it was in relation to those who were making fun of people who believed they could communicate with the dead. The trend of communicating with the dead was taking the nation by storm.

From 1850 to 1859, newspapers around the world reported on these "rappings" or "knockings" that were believed to have been noises made by deceased loved ones while they were being contacted by a medium. The medium would then interpret the noises and tell the living what the dead wanted them to know. Today, we would call this a séance. People would flock to the houses or storefronts of these mediums for a chance to "talk" to their loved ones. Trains often dedicated a particular car to a medium who would entertain travelers between destinations.

Quite as popular were those who tried to debunk what was happening. With the invention of electric lighting, more and more households were having it installed. This new invention was often blamed for the noises and strange shadows that would appear during a "rapping." The argument between belief and disbelief became nearly as popular as the séances themselves.

One of the debunkers was a believer first. The following article was published in the *Carroll Free Press* on April 23, 1852:

> *Confession of a Medium,—Benj. F. Cooley makes a statement through the* Springfield Republican *in regard to "spiritual rappings," in which he says: "Having had extended opportunities for the past three years to investigate the subject, I have arrived at what appears to me to be the true solution of the mystery. I now feel that compels me to speak out, and let my fellow men know what the results of my investigations are. In the first place, let me state that by the believers in these manifestations I have been considered a good 'medium,' that I have myself been a believer in the spiritual nature of these manifestations, and have very often believed that I was conversing with the spirits of the great men of earth, but who are now the great immortal in higher spheres. Now, my mind is entirely changed, and this change of mind has been produced by a long, deep, and earnest steady and investigation of the nature, power, and application of electrical or psychological changes, and of clairvoyance. All of these taken together, I find, will produce the same mysterious and startling phenomena that have already been produced throughout the country, and attributed to the operations of departed spirits."*

Perhaps Cooley was right; maybe the noises made by electricity combined with the desire to speak to the dead led folks to believe. But why was it so common all of a sudden? That was likely due to the newspaper reports. The more it was reported on, the more it happened. The *Carroll Free Press* reported in December 1852 that "rappings" had become so popular that "they have now become an everyday matter-of-fact thing." The article went on to tell of a woman so caught up in the rappings that she had supposedly communicated with her dead husband who had been poisoned. He told her that she, too, was being poisoned and she agreed, saying she had died at least twelve times already. This woman was committed by her friends and taken to the Ohio State Lunatic Asylum in Columbus. The same article in the *Carroll Free Press* that called rappings everyday occurrences also reported that the Ohio State Lunatic Asylum had twenty persons in its care who were there because of "insanity clearly traceable to spirit-rappings."

Artist's digital illustration of an old séance or "spiritual rapping." *Courtesy Bailey Lane.*

The *Cleveland Herald* published an article blaming the churches for focusing on only two things: either promoting the ability to speak to the dead or things such as the second coming. In 1831, a Baptist preacher by the name of William Miller was convinced that he had figured out the date of Christ's return. When the date came and went, he shifted his preaching to still include the second coming, just without a specific date. This preaching supposedly caused his followers to believe that if Christ could return a second time, so could their loved ones.

In April 1853, the Brooklyn Association of Congregational Ministers met to discuss the problem. Harriet Beecher Stowe's brother Reverend Charles Beecher reported on his findings after doing his own investigation. He felt that no one was intentionally trying to fool anyone, nor was it electrical or magnetic, and it was not the "unconscious involuntary mental action of a [living] person"; it was indeed a spirit. However, he did not believe it to be a "blest" spirit but a demonic one. The church wanted to hide his report at first, but his brothers Thomas and Henry pleaded his case, and the report was made public. This led to public outcry both for and against "Spiritual Rappings."

For several weeks, the editor of the *Carroll Free Press* and the local citizens went back and forth with published letters on the happenings. A correspondent for the paper, Mr. Argus, felt that the "spiritual manifestations" were a passing fad. He felt people had the right to believe in the manifestations or not. Whether they were figments of the imagination, or from God, or the devil, it did not matter, as they would soon be forgotten.

The very next article in the same paper was a letter defending the manifestations as real and complaining that Argus had no right to claim otherwise. A note from the editor states that they published the rebuttal letter because "we desire that the readers of the *Free Press* may have an opportunity of becoming posted on all subjects that agitate the public mind." The editor or editors also published something of a retraction stating that Argus should have done more research and "should have considered, that something more than an essay on humbug, and humbuggers in general" would not make people change their ways. They purported that Argus should have attended a rapping to find out for himself what was really happening.

A few weeks later, another letter to the editor appeared from Mr. A.R. Dempster, a concerned citizen of Leesburgh (now Leesville), who claimed that Argus was a fictitious name and that the real reporter should have called himself Mr. Prejudice. Dempster went on to say that the claims made by Argus were against adults who should know better than to fall for such things and that Dempster knew of an instance when children were also involved.

The account Dempster referred to was that of a "married lady of this town" who had gone to visit another friend named Mr. Roby. The lady had taken her nine-year-old daughter with her. This daughter and Roby's son, who was about the same age, and two other boys took a "working stand" (what we would call a Ouija board) and formed a circle around it. Soon thereafter, the knockings began. They claimed it was the deceased sister of the lady who had come to visit Roby. This spirit began "talking" to the people in the room by using the letters on the board. It told the lady she needed to leave the proslavery church. If the lady promised to leave, the "ghost" would let her go home. When asked for proof of the "ghost," the board lifted from the floor, twisted onto its side, flipped over, danced onto the carpet, and moved into four different rooms of the house before coming to rest in the lady's lap. This kept repeating late into the night, with the "ghost" continually asking the lady to promise to stop going to the church she was attending and the lady refusing. The lady asked if there was no gospel at the proslavery church, and the board shook violently and pointed to "no." The "ghost" then asked her to sing. She asked what she should sing, and the response was "I Would Not Live Always," so the lady sang the hymn. Finished singing, she told the others that she was indeed convinced that this was her deceased sister, as she had resolved earlier in the evening that if asked to sing that hymn, she would know. Since she had told no one of this, she knew the others had not spelled out that hymn on purpose. She then promised the "ghost" she would never return to the church she had been attending and would begin attending the antislavery church instead.

After retelling this to the editor, Dempster wrote, "Now, Mr. Editor, will you or Mr. Argus, inform your readers by what 'trick' Mr. Roby obtained a knowledge of what was passing in the mind of the lady in question? How did he know what conclusion she had come to in the secret recesses of her own heart?" Apparently, Dempster felt this was a compelling enough account to convince Argus that the knockings were real. That was not the case. Argus responded in the May newspaper by quoting the chief editor of the Cuyahoga newspaper. This was his response:

> *Then shall blockheads in the Jackassical dome of disclosive procedure, above the allfired great leatherfungus of Peter Nip-ninny go, the Gooseberry Grinder, rise into the dome of the disclosure, until co-equal and co-extensive and conglomerated lumuxes, in one comprehensive mux, shall assimilate into nothing and revolve like a bobtailed pussycat after the space where the tail was!*

It appears Argus was still not a believer, and as the editor had stated in a previous paper, he did indeed like to "agitate the public mind."

Whether it was indeed real or somehow faked, thousands of people around the world believed they could communicate with the dead in this manner. The fad seemed to fade out by the 1860s. Either that or the newspapers just got tired of reporting on it and moved to something else. As we know, séances did not die out completely. Ehrich Weiss, better known as Harry Houdini, and his wife, Bess, set out to debunk spiritualists after Sir Arthur Conan Doyle's wife claimed to have communicated with Ehrich's mother. Jean Doyle was supposedly inhabited by Mrs. Weiss, who then wrote a fifteen-page letter to Ehrich. Ehrich and Bess knew the letter could not be true because it was written in perfect English and talked about the cross of Jesus, something Ehrich's Hungarian Jewish mother would never have done. After that, Ehrich became somewhat obsessed with proving séances were fake. Others claim he was obsessed with trying to communicate with his mother. Whether it was proof or disproof that drove Ehrich, there was indeed an obsession.

Ehrich Weiss was not the only one to become overly obsessed. During the 1850s, mental institutions around the world were filling with people who had "gone mad" spending all their time and money attending these rappings, hoping to get answers from their dead loved ones. Nearly 175 years later, we still do not have the answers. Some still believe that ghosts are not real. Others believe they are very real. Another group feels they are real but are from a dark and sinister background. Whatever you may believe, this book was not written to prove or disprove their existence. It is simply an account of past encounters and hopefully, when possible, the story behind what may have happened to cause the dead to stay in a particular location.

CHAPTER 2

GHOSTLY SIGHTINGS AROUND THE COUNTY

When I first began researching ghost stories around Carroll County, I went to the internet and asked, "Okay, who wants to share their favorite local ghost story?" Several people responded, but typically just with quick anecdotes of what they had encountered. Stories like, "I grew up out on Apollo Road and would 100 percent smell cigarette smoke and no one in our house smoked. One day, I saw a shadow figure use our trash can when it was only me in the room. The place had caught fire several times, and there was other weird stuff that happened to my dad while trying to rebuild the house."

Another person shared, "There was a house in Harlem Springs that was a rental property. Renters kept moving out because of weird things happening. The television channel would randomly change. The dryer door would slam shut all night and various other things. Because renters kept moving out, the owner finally just tore the house down."

Joyce Foster shared with me about growing up on the family farm with all sorts of animals. She said her mother would sit at the table where she was able to look out the driveway. Many times, her mom talked about seeing the shadow of a farmer wearing bib overalls and a straw hat walking along the drive. They thought their mom was simply seeing things until one very sunny day when Joyce saw the shadow herself. She did some research and discovered that a former owner had passed away in the hay field. Her mother said there was no need to worry about him, as he was friendly.

Many people are like Joyce and her siblings and think that those who share these stories are crazy or just seeing things, until they see something themselves and then question what they really saw. Often, they want to tell their story but are afraid. Some know what they are seeing, but they do not want the stigma of being thought of as crazy. One person shared their story with me but asked that I not reveal who they are for that very reason. They lived in an older house in Carrollton proper and, after being in the house for about six months, realized the former owner was still there. At first, the previous owner tried to scare the family away by making the lights flicker and doors open and close on their own, and they could hear him walking up and down the stairs. Not fazed by these occurrences, the family was determined to stay. Apparently, the ghost realized this and gave up.

"My in-laws used to live in a house way back a long lane that they swore was haunted by an old man. One of the upstairs bedroom's lights would turn on after you heard footsteps in the hallway. It was on 164 between Kilgore and Amsterdam. I think that the Amish bought it." This story was shared by someone else.

There was another tale of some guys who had a little more trouble getting rid of their spirit. One of the guys had just purchased a house and had invited his buddies over for an evening around the fire. About four or five guys were sitting around just talking and having a good time when someone noticed that the porch swing was moving. No one was on the porch, no one had been on the porch, and there was no wind—not even a breeze. They knew this because the wind chimes above the swing were still. They ignored it and went on with their evening. One of the items they were burning was an old chair from the attic. It had been left by a previous owner and was falling apart.

One of the guys was sitting nearby watching and petting one of the dogs. The chair was not igniting. All thought this odd since it was so old and seemed quite brittle. Several minutes had gone by, and the chair was not even smoldering. The owner of the house poked at it with a stick and pushed more burning logs closer. Still, the chair did not want to burn. They waited a while longer and suddenly, as if someone had poured lighter fluid onto the chair, it ignited with a whoosh. In that same moment, the hair on the dog's back stood on end and became stiff. The guy petting the dog jerked away, and the dog let out a low growl and kept his eyes on the fire. This dog was not known to growl. As the flames from the finally burning chair whooshed again, it looked like something had leaped from the flames. The dog barked and took off after this shadow as it raced across a nearby field. The other three dogs followed suit. The owner finally got the dogs to return, but all four sat glaring into the field and refusing to move until nothing remained of the burning chair.

Because some folks were okay with their story being told, but not the location, you will have to bear with the vagueness at times. Their stories are just as good without the need for knowing where it took place. Becca Lynn shared her recollection: "My best friend growing up lived in a house in town. A long time ago a lady hanged herself in the tree outside my friend's bedroom window. We would sometimes see a shadow of a person hanging in that tree on certain nights."

Some folks were more than eager to share exactly where they experienced their ghost. Darci Starn shared this:

> There's a field in Amsterdam on an Apex back road that is haunted. A friend and I were walking up the path and saw someone standing a mile or so away. We turned around to walk back to the road and the next thing I know, not even 10 seconds later, he was standing right behind us. It was a young ghost soldier wearing an old bluish, I think, uniform like WWI maybe. He had the whole uniform on: hat, huge long gun, ammo strap going across his chest, everything. I was screaming and running as fast as I could and he's just effortlessly running next to me, staring me down the whole time, not taking his eyes off me. My friend and I jumped the ditch and onto the road and he was gone. Disappeared.

Another story was shared by Jonathan Lane, who had recently finished high school and was looking for something new to do in life. He was living in a rental house near Seventh Street. The move from Cincinnati to little old laid-back Carrollton was enough culture shock, but when he awoke one evening to find what he called the "Amish man" being pulled into the cabinet in his bedroom, it was quite startling. Jonathan said, "I was asleep and dreaming that an Amish man was being pulled into a cabinet in the corner of my bedroom by his feet. When I woke up, it was still happening!" It is quite possible that this visitor may not have been an Amish man but a man from the pioneer days. Quakers were quite prevalent in the surrounding area, and their dress from the 1800s is quite like the way the Amish dress today. Either way, Jonathan refused to stay in that house. It has been over twenty years, and he still has disturbing memories of waking to see this man either trying to climb out of the cabinet or being sucked in.

Dave Kean shared an experience he and some friends had when they were young. There is a ravine on the back part of the old Rutan farm, where Carrollton High School is now located. These boys would hike out and go camping along this ravine. On several occasions, they would look out and see strange lights in the direction of the Rutan farm. At first, they thought the lights must have been caused by cars on a nearby road. Try as they might, they could not get any of their own vehicles to re-create the strange lighting. It would not have been so odd if the ravine was not so deep and they had not been able to see the house lights once they climbed the hill. They even checked to see if the lights from the house were reflecting off something but found nothing. The strange lights at the top of the hill only seemed to appear on the nights they were all camping.

Others were a little more in-depth, such as Brenda Galliher's story:

I lived in a house outside of Carrollton when I was in elementary school. We would hear footsteps on the wood stairs, doors opening and closing, and one time I was sleeping with my left leg hanging off my bed and something ran a finger from the heel of my foot to the toe. There was no one in the house at the time except me. Everyone else was outside and we had no indoor pets. My leg was not low enough for it to be a rodent, so…no other explanation. I never saw anything because when it was dark, I always kept my eyes closed for fear I WOULD see something. We moved from there when I was 11, but to this day, I will not sleep with an appendage hanging over the edge.…I'm in my fifties! It scarred me for life!

Brenda continued:

That house had a lot of unexplained noises. Footsteps on the stairs was the big one. The stairs didn't have carpet or anything so the footsteps were not muffled, and no one showed up at the top of the stairs. I can't tell you how many times that happened. There was a door at the bottom of the stairs that my mom would close after we went to bed because she stayed up watching TV. My sister and I would talk and carry on, and my mom would open the door, pound on the stairs with the wooden paddle and tell us to settle down and go to sleep. There were times when the door didn't open, but we could hear the paddle on the steps and since we hadn't been loud, we would yell to her and ask why she was pounding on the stairs. She didn't answer, so we yelled louder. A few seconds later, we would hear

Artist's rendition of a spooky figure in an oil field. *Janice Lane collection.*

the door open, and Mom would inquire about why we were yelling, tell us she didn't pound on the stairs and to go to sleep.

There was one bedroom downstairs in the house that we were afraid to go into. Up until the time we moved (we lived there nine or ten years), I only remember going in that room a handful of times except when Mom was in there. Even then I didn't go in there much. It was creepy, and I'm not sure why it was so scary, but I didn't like it at all. I didn't like the closet in my room or my parents' room either. (They didn't have doors.) But the day I felt something touch my foot…wow!

Someone else shared their experience while working at one of the oil fields:

It was very late at night. Sometime between 1:00 a.m. and 5:00 a.m. I was working in the back lot in what we called the company man's trailer. It was in the back of the lot, the furthest away from everything else. It was the lot where cars parked during the day. I was in this shack all alone. Just me and the hum of the rig. I happened to look out the window and there was a man standing several feet away staring back at me. I didn't think anything of it at first but then realized something was off. He didn't seem to have any lower body. There was something about him, even though I couldn't see him well, that made me think he was Honduran. He was wearing a Bob the Builder–type hat, so I assumed he was an oil worker, but he also had these jet-black hollow eyes that really had no definition to them.

I went outside onto the metal deck, and he didn't move. He just stood or, well, hovered there, staring back at me. I wasn't really scared, just bothered. So, I went back inside, picked up a magazine and refused to look out again. Later, I did some research and learned that a worker had been killed at a nearby oil pad. He was of a Middle Eastern background. I'm not sure why he would show up at our pad, but I'm fairly certain that's who I saw.

I told one of the company men about my strange encounter, and he said there had been a lot of strange things happening at that pad. Bits would break that should not have. The generator lights would go off for no reason. Lots of strange things.

The pad is closed now.

Yet another story was shared by Ronata Phillips, who grew up in an old brick farmhouse on Channel Road. The house was built around 1960 or 1970 to replace the house that had been on the property but was destroyed by fire. Yet something weird was happening in this newer home. At night, Ronata would get up to use the restroom downstairs, and when she tried to climb the stairs to return to her room, it was as if something picked her up and carried her up the stairs. "It is hard to explain, but it was like I kinda flew somehow." She shared that it happened on several occasions. There were other times when she would feel someone shake her awake, but when she opened her eyes, no one else was in the room. Her sister hated the upstairs but never told Ronata why. She, too, may have experienced these strange things but did not want to talk about them. Ronata said that she also would wake up knowing things that she should have no way of knowing. "It is hard to explain; I just knew stuff. I wouldn't know it, then like, I would wake up and know stuff. I would know stuff about my parents that I had no business knowing. It was creepy and weird at the same time." It was like the ghost was telling her things in her sleep.

Ronata also talked about other things that happened on that property. Somehow, she knows there was a body buried in the silo but had no way of proving it. She does not believe that whoever is buried there is the one haunting the house. Whoever, or whatever, is haunting the house is much more sinister. Her mother had a priest come and bless the property on multiple occasions. It would keep this dark spirit away for a while, but it always seemed to come back.

Many more encounters like these are out there but will need to wait until another time. The next twelve chapters beckon us to delve deeper into the depths of actual haunted buildings. Brace yourself as we leave behind the brief encounters and step into the tangible reality of eerie abodes, steeped in history, their rooms laden with the weight of unquiet spirits and haunting secrets waiting to be unraveled.

CHAPTER 3

BELL-HERRON MIDDLE SCHOOL

While one might assume that the innocence of youth would be enough to keep the supernatural at bay, many mediums will tell you that ghosts often like to be where there is a lot of energy. What better place for a lot of energy than a middle school? Built for the 1926–27 school year as the high school, this building would become the Bell-Herron Middle School in September 1982 and would serve that purpose until it was razed in 2019. For ninety-two years, this building was a hub of activity. Not only did it house various grade levels over the years, but its auditorium served as gymnasium, cafeteria, study hall, and theater. It was not surprising to discover a few unseen tenants residing there.

A former teacher shared an encounter they had late one evening upon returning to the school to retrieve some forgotten homework. The teacher's son had visited their classroom earlier in the day, and as they prepared for bed, the son remembered that he had left his homework on this teacher's desk. Despite being in pajamas, the two drove to the school and hurried to the classroom. Try as they might, the door would not unlock. The teacher was becoming more agitated and even more annoyed when the son suggested calling on the ghost to help. They wondered what he was talking about when the son yelled, "George! Come open the door!" With no key in the lock, the door opened.

Another story was that of a teacher cleaning her room. She had placed a bucket in the sink to fill with water. She turned to get a rag, and when she turned back, the bucket was lifting from the sink. It moved out of the sink,

Carrollton High School, built in 1913. It would later be renamed the Bell-Herron Middle School and be host to numerous unseen inhabitants. *Janice Lane collection.*

over the edge and spilled everywhere. She ran from the room and went to the school office. The vice principal was still there, and when she told him what had happened, he laughed and told her he was surprised she had not met the ghosts earlier. The vice principal did not respond to requests to elaborate on that statement.

After my own encounter in May 2015, I am not surprised that he did not want to share anything he may have experienced. Something like this makes you question your own sanity. We had been busily preparing for weeks, rehearsing and setting up the stage for the junior high musical. It was closing night, and the building was buzzing with parent volunteers, teachers, and students, each occupying their designated roles. My responsibility for the evening was to oversee the concessions, and as I made my way through the dimly lit expanse of the multipurpose room, I suddenly felt a tug on one of my belt loops. Startled, I turned to find the source of the sensation, only to find myself completely alone. Perplexed, I looked around the room, half expecting mischievous students playing a prank, but there was no one to be found. There was not a soul in sight and not a single obstacle in the uninhabited room, save for a few wrestling mats tucked away in a distant corner.

I shrugged it off and went on to the concession area, only to find the cooler, where everything was stored, was locked. Frustrated, I turned to go back and ask if anyone had the key. As I reentered the multipurpose room, a janitor I had not met before smiled and offered to show me his trick for opening the cooler. I followed him back to the concessions area and the cooler. I expected him to have a key, but instead, he told me to push on one side of the door and pull on the other. The cooler opened. I turned to thank him, but he had already moved on. It seemed a little odd that he had not used a key and that he had trusted me with the knowledge of how to open it. The thought quickly left as I continued preparing for the evening. I had also forgotten about the strange tug on my belt loop.

Two hours later, the show had ended, and we were cleaning up. Most of the children and their parents had gone. A few of us stayed and were cleaning and playing around. I noticed the janitor from earlier and went to thank him for helping with the cooler and for volunteering to work so late on a weekend. He was standing near a wall in the corner of the room, and when I thanked him, he said he was just doing his job. I could not help but express my surprise at not having met him before, considering I believed I was familiar with all the janitorial staff. He smiled and told me that he was the night janitor. To make small talk, I made a reference to how it must be kind of weird there at night. He grinned and replied, "You have no idea. Did you meet the little red-haired girl?"

My brow wrinkled, and I wondered who he meant.

He continued to smile. "She bumped into you earlier, didn't she?"

"What are you talking about?" I wondered how he could know about the tug I'd felt on my belt loops.

"She told me."

"She told you?" Now I was starting to think that maybe he had a daughter who had come to work with him and was not supposed to be there. Maybe she had run away, afraid that I would report him for bringing his daughter.

Before I could formulate any other thoughts on this, he continued: "She lives here now. Most people can't see her, but many have sensed her presence. She likes it here with all the other children."

Goosebumps formed on my arms. I could see the other moms cleaning up and having fun out of the corner of my eye and felt a little guilty for not helping. Another part of me wanted to run, but the part of me that wanted to hear what else he had to say stayed firmly planted.

"What little girl are you talking about?" I was almost afraid to have him answer.

He simply smiled and went on to tell me how she was very afraid when she first showed up at the Bell-Herron Middle School, and to help calm her down, he would leave a coloring book and crayons on a desk in the basement dressing room. As he talked, my gut churned, the hair on my arms stood on end, and I wondered what I had really encountered earlier in the evening. He also told me that there were other ghosts living there as well, and he had brought in a Bible for one of them. I wanted to know more, but we were interrupted by someone calling my name. I turned to see another mom waving to me. I turned to excuse myself, and once again, he vanished, just like he had earlier by the cooler.

I went to see what the other mom had wanted when I noticed our usual janitor, Tom. I told him I had missed his help all evening and asked what the other janitor's name was. Tom gave me a funny look and asked, "What other janitor?" I was beginning to think they were all pulling a trick on me. As I explained what had happened, Tom argued that he was the only janitor on duty. I gave up and went home.

The next day, my daughter and I were discussing the night before, and I told her about my conversation with the mysterious janitor. My daughter said she had seen him and thought she had a picture of me talking to him. I was beginning to feel a little better since she had seen him too. She pulled out her cellphone and showed me the pictures she had taken. None of them were great, since it was an early cellphone and she was only thirteen. There was one of me standing by the wall, but I was alone. She shook her head and argued that he had to be in that photo; she had seen him. Yet I was clearly by myself. It is quite possible that this janitor was very real and just happened to be elusive enough to avoid the camera, but it is odd that no one else seemed to know him and I could not find him in any yearbooks, past or present.

Shyanne Kirkpatrick, the granddaughter of one of the other janitors, said she was hanging out in the building one evening waiting on her grandpa to finish cleaning. To the best of her knowledge, they were the only two people in the building. She was on the third floor, running up and down the hallway, while her grandpa was downstairs somewhere. A janitor's cart was sitting in the middle of the hallway, and she could hear it squeak every time it moved. "I must've run past that cart ten to fifteen times. Every time I did, it moved a little and the wheels squeaked. The cart was very loud. I went to use the restroom at the end of the hall, and when I was finished, I couldn't open the door. I yelled for help about a dozen times, but no one could hear me. I tried for several minutes before I was finally able to squeeze out. The janitor's cart had been shoved against the door, and the brakes were on." She wondered how a cart that was so noisy could have made its way down the hallway, with its brake on, and held the door shut with no one around. She called for

Left: This photo is blurry, as it was taken by my then thirteen-year-old daughter on a cellphone. I'm in the white sweater, on the far left, clearly by myself—although I swore I was talking to the night janitor. *Courtesy Bailey Lane.*

Below: The Bell-Herron Middle School just before it was razed. *Janice Lane collection.*

help again once she got out, but there was still no answer. There was also a sudden, severe coldness in the air. A chill came over her, so she ran down the stairs to her grandpa. He swore there was no one else in the building. One wonders if it was maybe the mysterious janitor I met. After hearing the teacher who shared her story about the bucket lifting on its own and Shyanne's encounter with the janitor's cart, it begs the question: is there a mysterious janitor ghost who used to continue cleaning even after his death? Since the building was razed, we will likely never know.

Because ghosts like energy, it is hard to say where the ones went that once resided at the Bell-Herron Middle School. Perhaps they followed the students to the new building on Scio Road. Or maybe they stayed close by and are visiting the homes on Fourth Street behind the old Bell-Herron. Something else we will likely never know…

CHAPTER 4

ALLER FARM

There is a strong possibility that the ghost who assisted in opening a locked classroom door at the Bell-Herron Middle School might not have been directly connected to that location. It is known that certain spirits have the tendency to attach themselves to objects or individuals, although the exact reasons behind this phenomenon remain uncertain. It is believed that the innocence of young children makes them particularly vulnerable to such attachments. This may explain the connection between the teacher's son and the spirit called George, as well as George's willingness to lend a hand in opening the locked door. While the house at the Aller farm had been in their family for years, and they had visited often, it was only after they moved in that the young man started experiencing George's presence. He also mentioned the existence of another, less amicable spirit in the house. The encounter with this darker spirit left the young man gripped with fear, leading him to actively avoid its presence. He was grateful that it was not a frequent visitor. On the other hand, George became a source of friendship and companionship for the family. Described as a "yellow man with an ethereal quality," George seemed to enjoy rearranging objects within the house. Books would inexplicably dislodge themselves from the shelves and television remotes would levitate and then drop to the floor, and even when no one else was present, George would roll marbles down the stairs, leaving them scattered at the bottom for the family to discover upon their return home.

When asked how they knew the ghost's name was George, the son shrugged and said he was not sure. He felt like someone had maybe told him that it was George and that George had built the house they lived in. He thought that he had heard somewhere there was some aggravation on George's part because George had a dream that he needed to move the house and so he did. His wife was very upset with him for moving the house, so she took the children and left.

The history of the farm was traced back, and it was learned that the property had changed owners many times over the years but usually within the same family. It was not surprising to discover that a man named George had indeed owned the property at one time. His name was George Hershel Aller. He and his wife, Jane Marshall Butler Aller, had acquired the farm upon the death of George's father, Absalom Aller.

Tragedy struck George and Marsha (as she was known, according to her obituary) Aller when both of their daughters succumbed to tuberculosis within months of each other in 1900. After this devastating loss, George and Marsha relocated to Hudson, Ohio. However, tragedy struck once again when George unexpectedly passed away due to a heart attack. His remains were returned to Carrollton, where he was laid to rest in Grandview Cemetery. This fit with the story of George losing his family and moving, but not in the same way my friend remembered hearing it. Had the correct George been found?

Further investigation revealed the actual lineage of ownership for the farm. Prior to George inheriting the property from his father, Absalom Aller had received ownership from his own father, John Aller. John Aller had purchased the farm from an Andrew Moore. The farm had been purchased by Andrew Moore, predating 1825, when the land was still a part of Columbiana County. John Aller purchased the farm from Andrew Moore after marrying Mary Christina Kintner. John and Mary would raise ten children on the farm. One of those ten children, and Absalom's brother, was named George. George never married, and there is no record of him living on the farm as an adult.

George owned a small farm in Hocking County, but when he died in 1847, records say he was buried on the family farm beside his father, who had passed a year earlier. The family burial plot was known as the Aller Family Cemetery and was marked by a stone wall and iron gate fence. A few years later, when Absalom and George's brother Daniel lost his one-year-old son Lewis F., he, too, was buried in the little cemetery. It would be nearly twenty years before the cemetery was used again, at least according to

The Aller Family Cemetery, date unknown. *Courtesy the Carroll County Genealogical Society.*

kept records. Mary Christina was buried there in 1875, followed by another grandson, Robert Elmer, in 1879. Robert Elmer was one of Absalom's sons.

It is unclear how the elder George died. His will is dated October 14, 1847. He would die four days later. It seems he wrote his will almost as if he knew he were going to die. Unfortunately, county death records do not go back that far, so we do not know what caused George's death. It is possible he had an uncurable disease such as hepatitis, and if he is indeed the George who has been haunting my young friend, that is why he appears to be yellow.

According to Mary Christina's obituary, she was the sixth family member to be buried in this little cemetery. We know of John, George, Lewis F., Robert, and Christina, but who was number six? And with a gap of twenty years, were there others?

Also odd, if you search for George's and his father John's graves online, you will find two listings. One lists them as buried here in the family cemetery, and the other shows them in Grandview Cemetery in Carrollton. How can there be two burial sites with the exact same information? Because at some point, their stones were moved.

Over the course of the following century, ownership of the farm changed many times. Regrettably, some time before the 1960s, someone made the unfortunate decision to remove the gravestones and stone wall that marked the cemetery's location on the farm. According to a 1963 news article, only

George Aller's stone now standing near the fence in Grandview Cemetery. *Courtesy Richard Culler.*

three stones were recovered: those belonging to George; his father, John; and little Lewis. Thanks to an Eagle Scout, the stones were taken to Grandview Cemetery and placed near the fence line after being discovered in the barn. Because there are records of the Aller Family Cemetery and records for Grandview, these three stones were listed in both. However, it is important to note that while the gravestones were moved, there is no evidence to suggest that the actual graves were relocated. Perhaps this was the move George was so opposed to, as it disrupted the resting place of his loved ones.

Once the stones were discovered in the bottom of the barn, people started talking and pointing fingers. The records on file for this cemetery at the Carroll County Genealogical Library contain a letter from a previous owner stating that they were completely unaware of a cemetery having ever been on their property. They asked that if a location could be found, to please let them know and they would mark the area with a fence or something. Since no fence exists, they either never found the location or decided not to mark it. My friend and his family (who came to own the property years after the letter writer) were completely unaware of this cemetery ever existing. They, too, would like to know its exact whereabouts. The current owners did not respond to inquiries about any strange happenings or sightings or knowledge of a cemetery on their property. For fear of trespassing, no one has gone out to investigate the actual site. The land has changed considerably over the years from farming and landscaping, so without expensive equipment and any living soul able to tell, it is unlikely the exact location will ever be found. Since the Aller family's ownership, the once extremely large farm has been broken down into smaller parcels, and some are even parts of public property. This is another good reason to let the mysterious graves rest in peace. Maybe someday the opportunity will present itself and the cemetery's actual location will be pinpointed.

CHAPTER 5

BLUEBIRD FARM PARK

Meet Clem. Apparently, this ghost is not camera shy. Or is it just the power of suggestion? I was completely alone while taking photos at this location, and nothing out of the ordinary showed on the camera screen. It was not until they were being downloaded unto the computer that something seemed amiss. In the small pavilion next to the house, my daughter pointed out that something appeared to have moved. It might have been a shadow, or it is quite possible I moved when taking the photos. But when you look at the first photo and then the second, it is evident that there is suddenly something in the middle section that is not in the first photo.

The same thing seemed to happen with the upstairs window of the main house. It might have been a strange reflection from the trees, but it certainly transformed from a weird shadow into the face of a man to me, and images in windows are difficult to confirm or deny when seeking ghosts.

Several former employees had suggested investigating the Bluebird Farm Park and mentioned that the ghost's name was Clyde or Clem. It was believed that he was the son of a previous owner and would create noises around the house. He expressed disapproval when the house was transformed from a private residence into a tearoom. Some employees even reported smelling pipe tobacco when there was no one else present. One witness claimed to have seen a man dressed in Civil War attire emerging from the basement storage area and ascending the stairs. When asked how they came to know the ghost's name was Clem, no one could provide a definite answer. Similar to George, it was just known to them.

The Bluebird Farm House built in 1849 by Jacob Kintner, whose son still roams through the basement. *Janice Lane collection.*

A sign in the parking lot says the property was established in 1816, sixteen years before Carroll County was even established. According to the Land Office Records, Christian Kintner purchased the land from then U.S. President James Monroe. Christian and his wife, Elizabeth, purchased 150 acres at five dollars an acre. There they would build a log home and raise their ten children. In 1834, Christian's sister Mary Christina and her husband, John Aller, purchased a farm nearby. Ten years later, in 1844, Christian sold part of the land to his sons Jacob, Abraham, Jonas, and Christian Jr. The boys had all reached adulthood and were ready to begin their own families. Jacob bought the western half of the property near the current sewage treatment plant and Christian Jr. the east half, which would now be between Grandview Cemetery and the county airport. The land where the current high school, industrial park, and Jo-Mac now sit was sold to Abraham and Jonas.

Five years later, Jacob married Louisa Kintner (a first cousin), and they lived in the log cabin for sixteen years before building the brick house that still stands on the property. *J.H. Beers' Commemorative Biographical Record of the Counties of Harrison and Carroll* called it "a fine brick residence and commodious out-buildings." While Christian Jr., Abraham, and Jonas eventually sold their share of the property, Jacob and Louisa lived out their days on the farm. They had eleven children. Jacob died in 1907 and Louisa in 1911. As requested in Jacob's will, the farm was auctioned off after Louisa's death, and each of his living children and grandchildren received a portion of the money.

Their oldest son, Benjamin, married Lavinia Elizabeth Hawk, and they raised their children on a farm nearby. Their second son, Clement, owned a farm just north of his parents and across the road from his aunt and uncle, the Allers. Clement never married and seemed constantly drawn to the family farm. In February 1879, a news article recounts Clement and his brother Isaac embarking on a boat journey from Steubenville, Ohio, to Kansas City, Missouri. They returned home by March. Apparently, they did not like being so far away from Carrollton. Clement suffered from bouts of melancholy, another likely reason he did not stay in Missouri. An article published in the *Carroll Free Press* on Wednesday, August 10, 1898, reports that Clement went to visit his parents, accompanied by one of his brothers. The article further reveals that after exhibiting "despondent spirits for some weeks due to ill health," Clement left the premises unnoticed, wielding a pair of pointed scissors. He secluded himself in a serene spot and made two desperate attempts to plunge the scissors into his chest with the intention of ending his own life. One of the wounds was very serious. He was in a feeble state when the family discovered him, and Dr. Aldridge was summoned and ultimately saved Clement's life. Although he recuperated from his wounds, Clement apparently continued to suffer from his depression. When his mother died and the farm was sold off, Clement purchased the shares of his siblings. Clem lived out his days on the farm with his niece Ila Abrahims. Having failing health, he sold the farm to John C. Beck in 1939 and relocated to the county home, now the Golden Age Retreat. A few months later, on October 6, 1940, he finally succumbed to death and was buried in Grandview Cemetery. This cemetery sits adjacent to the family farm and is the same cemetery where the Aller family gravestones were moved.

Beck lived in the house for four years before selling it to the LePine family in 1943. They lived there until 1964, when they sold to Lewis Adams. Over the years, the property was broken down into various parcels, and pieces were sold off. Richard and Joyce Hannon bought the remaining fifty-five acres in 1972 and lived there until 1987. But they did not sell the property. Instead, they were the ones who turned the beautiful old, brick house into a tearoom. As mentioned earlier, employees said that Clem was apparently very unhappy about this decision. He would move things around and cause all kinds of trouble for Joyce. Dolls from her daughter's collection would be

The pavilion that sits to the left of the house. *Janice Lane collection.*

The same pavilion seconds later. Something is now in the middle section. *Janice Lane collection.*

moved, despite being in a locked case. Others complained of cold spots, even when sitting or standing beside the fireplace. There were times when unexplained noises would be heard, like footsteps in rooms no one was in or doors closing on their own. None of these things seemed to bother Joyce, as she continued to transform the house into a tearoom and remodel the rest of the property.

Over the next decade, the pre–Civil War barns were restored and transformed into a private residence, a gift shop, and three museums. Across the creek, in 2003, the Bluebird Farm Amphitheater was constructed, as well as stairs from the creek to the farmhouse and entrance roads. The grand opening was held on May 12, 2007. In 2008, Joyce Hannon donated the land and all the buildings to the Carroll County Park District. She passed away shortly after in January 2009.

The tearoom changed hands several times. Many restaurants were attempted and failed. No one knows the exact reason why nothing has been able to stay in business here. Since Joyce's death, former employees have continued to tell stories of seeing Clem and a second ghost wandering around. Clem seemed to like the basement and would often be "seen" in the storage room. A former employee who worked in the house while it was JB Chops Steakhouse said she witnessed lights that would turn on by themselves, and doors would close when no one was around. Other former employees from the other restaurants told of similar events.

Jen Minor, one of the former employees, had just begun working at the Bluebird Farm Park. She had been hired as an administrative assistant and was working alone long after the park had closed. The door chime had been unplugged for the day, and the doors were locked. She was on the third floor of the office/gift shop building when she heard someone talking. Curious, she went down to the second floor and could not find anyone, so she went to the basement. Still, there was no one around. She returned to the third floor and went back to work, but she again heard a woman talking. Racing down the steps a second time, she saw a woman dressed in a red outfit with a matching red hat go by the window. Jen looked out, and the woman was gone. Several days later, Jen saw a picture of Joyce Hannon and realized it was Joyce who had passed by the window. Apparently, Clem is not the only one who does not want to leave the beautiful home.

Since Joyce's appearance, no one has experienced anything too strange. Joyce likes to keep an eye on things and continues to ensure that business is running smoothly, while Clem stays in the basement section of the house. Sightings of Joyce seem to happen more on the grounds than in the buildings.

One of the most recent sightings was a manager who turned from his work to see Joyce standing beside him, watching. Apparently, he is doing a good job, since nothing bad or sinister seems to happen.

It would seem that Joyce was not bothered by Clem's spirit while she was alive because she, too, had a deep affection for the Bluebird Farm Park. She either overlooked his ornery ways or simply put up with them. Or maybe she was indeed annoyed and became a ghost herself to spite Clem. Yet another mystery we are not able to solve.

CHAPTER 6
THE COX MANSION

When anyone discusses haunted houses in Carroll County, the first to be mentioned is always the Cox Mansion. The massive brick house was built in 1887 by Isaac Cox for his wife, Lydia Ann Pottorf Cox. It was the largest brick house in the area for its time. Legend says that Isaac Cox built the elaborate house to appease his father-in-law, Henry Pottorf, who felt his daughter was marrying beneath her status. Rumors claim that Isaac overheard someone on their wedding day say that Lydia was not going to as fine a house as she was leaving, and he determined then and there to build her a suitable home. Legend also has it that her father told her that if Cox did not build her a home with all the luxuries a woman could ever want, she was free to return home. It should be noted that the couple had been married for twenty-seven years and most of their children had left home before the home was built. It was also eighteen years after her father's death, and ground was broken for the new home just a few weeks after Lydia's mother passed. Lydia's mother, Mary Hewitt Pottorf, died on April 13, 1887. In her will, dated March 19, 1878, Mrs. Pottorf states, "Item 2nd Having given to my daughter Lydia A. Cox all that I intend her to have, she is not to receive anything out of my Estate." It does sound as though there was some animosity between Lydia and her family. Whatever feelings there were between them, one will never know. It does seem odd that such an elaborate house would be constructed after Lydia's parents died and after having lived on the property for so many years. Isaac acquired the land in 1863 from his brother John, who had purchased it through a sheriff's sale

The Cox Mansion in all its glory with the family of Frank and Katie Cox in the front yard. *Courtesy Ken Lucas.*

following their father's unfortunate passing. It had gone to sheriff's sale after John sued the rest of the family for the rights to the property. It seems odd that he would then relinquish it to his brother just a few years later.

This is possibly when the mysteries of the land began. According to James's obituary posted in the *Carroll Free Press* on Thursday, May 22, 1856, he had been "for some months laboring under a disease of the spine, which produced occasional insanity." This disease was blamed as the cause of James hanging himself in the barn. Yet none of the ghost stories ever mention anything happening in the barn. The stories all seem to be associated with the mansion.

Isaac's decision to build such a magnificent home was likely influenced by various factors that will remain a mystery. The mansion was built fifty feet from the original clapboard house. But like any house that is built so elaborately and then finds itself empty time and time again, tales began to develop.

The Cox Mansion was certainly that kind of house. The twenty-room mansion sat atop one of the highest elevations in the county. It took four kilns on site of the 184-acre farm to make the bricks from a vein of clay just a half mile from the house. It took over a year for one hundred men who were paid one dollar a day to build the home. It was rumored that Cox had installed indoor plumbing, and instead of the traditional pot-bellied stoves for heat, he had a fireplace built in every room. Katie Cox, a daughter-in-law who lived in the house, was interviewed by Velma Griffin in 1978. Katie, then ninety-one and a half years old, said there were fireplaces in the living room and the kitchen only. The house had no other heat, and there was no indoor plumbing. Katie also told Velma she did not believe in ghosts, but there were times when she would hear the organ playing when no one was in the room. During the five years she lived in the house, she would often hear someone rap on the door twelve times at the stroke of midnight. She was convinced it was one of her boys sneaking out at night to try to scare her. The only time this did not happen was a night when her brother came to stay and had to catch a train at 2:00 a.m. Her sons denied the rapping on the door and claimed they would see a man out in the yard calling, "Come on, boys!" She never heard it or saw the man. Katie truly believed her own sons were just pulling pranks.

Living in a house of such splendor during a time when most folks lived in simple homes or log cabins was sure to elicit tall tales. The interior woodwork was all made from different types of wood found on the property. One news article said that each room had a different type of wood. They included walnut, cherry, white ash, chestnut, oak, and red elm, each of which took three months to cure in the sun before it could be used. The most talked-about piece was the thirty-seven-step spiral staircase that wound its way up three stories to the top of the sixty-foot tower on the southwest corner. Its banisters were made from black walnut, and it had no visible supports. Wall niches on the left held graceful statues.

Thirty-six windows gave tenants multiple views of the surrounding countryside. The carved stone window arches and the circular windows in the tower were the work of an English artisan. Some claim that on a clear day, you could see the Ohio River from the tower window that faced southwest. Donna Tucker remembers climbing those tower stairs as a young girl and said that if they had used binoculars, she believes they could have seen the river.

Rumors of a tunnel that ran from the house to the cement barn were numerous. Some say you can see the area where the tunnel ran from the air because of an indentation in the ground. A 1967 aerial photo of the farm does show an indentation, or maybe just a path, from the house

A photo of the spiral staircase with one of the recesses taken at the Cox Mansion in the 1960s. *Velma Griffin collection, courtesy the Carroll County Genealogical Society.*

toward the barn. The tunnel itself was rumored as having been used to help runaway slaves. This, however, is not true, since the house was built nearly twenty years after slavery ended. The tunnel turned out to be a coal bin that would be filled during the summer months when the wagons could make it up the steep hills. This was verified by William Cox, a grandson of Isaac's, in his interview with Velma Griffin. He said his dad, Seymour Cox, used to tell how the wagons, which were pulled by oxen, struggled to bring even a load of sand up the hill while the house was being built. The first load was so heavy the men stopped and dumped some sand off at a location midway up the drive. After that, the oxen would just automatically stop there with every load.

Upon completion of the house, it is said that Cox walked out the front door, turned, looked at his bride, and said, "Here is your house, dear," and then promptly fell dead. Others claim he committed suicide, but that may just be misinformation passed down, since it is known that his father was the one who died that way. Isaac Cox did die suddenly, but six years after the house was completed. On October 27, 1895, a surgeon was summoned from Pittsburgh, but it was too late to save Mr. Cox's life. He died due to peritonitis from a ruptured appendix. His widow, Lydia, remained in the house until her death in 1915. That is when their youngest son, Frank, and his wife, Katie, took over care of the house. They sold it in the 1920s to Joseph Hunter, and for the first time in nearly one hundred years, the farm was no longer in the possession of a Cox family member.

Joseph H. Hunter worked as a manager for the Pittsburgh Light Company and in 1906 founded the Detroit Insulated Wire Company. That factory had a daily output of one million feet of insulated wiring and was a major contributor to the Allied Forces during World War I. By the time Hunter purchased the Cox Mansion, he was said to have a net worth of $20 million. He was only twenty-one. It was also the 1920s, which was a time known for the wealthy throwing extravagant parties. Hunter set about making the mansion a showplace. It was then that indoor plumbing and newly invented central heating were installed. A steam plant was built on the property to provide the heat. Hunter had the central heating installed because fireplaces were not sufficient to heat such large rooms with such high ceilings. The master bedroom is said to have been twenty-four feet by twenty-four feet. A parlor with an entrance to the north and another to the south with a bay window was thirty-five feet by fifteen feet. The kitchen was twenty feet by twenty feet, and the hall that housed the spiral staircase was nine feet by nine feet.

Hunter furnished the home with Persian rugs, ornate furniture, and other housewares shipped in from Detroit, Michigan, and an interior decorator from Philadelphia was hired to oversee the final touches. Hunter hired Anson McVay as a caretaker (although some records indicate McVay was a co-owner) and Earl Fox as the chauffeur. Delco lighting was installed at this time as well.

In 1978, Earl Fox was interviewed about his time in the house. He confirmed the additions and renovations, and he also said that Hunter often held dinner parties for guests from Detroit and Pittsburgh, as well as local friends and neighbors. These parties often required ten to twelve servants and lasted for days. An additional six-room building was constructed at the rear of the mansion to provide a place for the servants. Fox claimed that none of the haunting stories were true; they were just tales spread by those who were jealous that they had not been invited to the elegant parties.

By the 1930s, the house sat vacant. It was about this time the stories of strange sounds, sights, and occurrences grew more abundant. Reportedly, a young woman had committed suicide in one of the bedrooms during one of Hunter's grand parties. At night, you could see her floating along the spiral staircase playing a violin. Others said they never saw the girl but could hear

The Cox Mansion in 1960. *Courtesy Dave Freshley.*

the violin playing. When the house was still standing, investigators claim the violin music was simply wind blowing down the tall spiral staircase from a knothole in the tower's woodwork. They claimed a bird had built a nest in the tower, and when the wind blew from the northeast, it would blow across a hair in the nest and vibrate just like a violin. Other stories from this period say that stringing horsehair across a hole in the attic of a house was common practice to keep thieves away.

There are numerous legends surrounding a brick with a woman's foot imprint that was once present in the house. Some say it was discovered in the attic, while others say it was along the stairwell. According to theories, the imprint was created when a woman either walked barefoot across the scorching brick after it was taken out of a kiln or was tragically thrown into the kiln itself. It was said that on certain nights, one could hear her anguished cries of pain.

Another story claimed that there was an unerasable bloodstain on the hardwood floor of one of the bedrooms. This was believed to have been made when someone carelessly spilled vermillion red paint during Hunter's renovation. Others claim the stain was made by the blood spilled by a man who slit his own throat in the bedroom. No reports of such an incident were found outside of the hearsay.

Legends circulated about doors mysteriously opening without any apparent cause. One explanation suggested that it was simply the weight of the door, considering they were three inches thick, mounted on three sturdy hinges and equipped with hand-forged latches. The sheer heft of such doors might have caused them to swing open on their own. However, this hypothesis raises the question of how the doors managed to close by themselves.

An early mystery associated with the house was that of one of the one hundred men hired to build it. The hired men slept in the barn. Each day, a man would count as the men headed to work and then count them again as they retired to the barn. One day, someone was missing. His name was John Koches, and he had come from Czechoslovakia in 1885 with his twelve-year-old son, Andrew, to Cleveland, Ohio. Koches spoke very little English. When he took the job to help build the Cox Mansion, he was allowed to bring his son with him. The son earned his keep by carrying water for the workers. On the day in question, the son appeared for work, but Koches was nowhere to be found. He had simply vanished overnight. The men scoured the countryside, but no trace of him was ever found. The son was sent back to Cleveland to live in an orphanage. Years later, Andrew would return to Augusta to try to find answers. Years after that, his son Joe would also return to the Cox Mansion, but still no answers were found. Oddly, no newspapers recorded this disappearance, and very little is known of the family. According to Andrew's obituary, he did not come to America until 1895, eight years after the house was built. This only deepens the mystery. Were the records wrong? Did he and his father come earlier? Or did it even happen at all? Maybe John Koches did work on the house and vanish, but of his own free will. Or maybe he fell victim to ill will. Perhaps the ghost seen pushing a wheelbarrow across the yard was Koches.

A well-known story among the family was the death of an adult family member who was bitten by a rabid dog. Prior to the discovery of the rabies vaccine, being bitten by an infected animal was frequently a death sentence for the victim. Supposedly, the family member was locked into one of the bedrooms and cared for until the time of his death. The identity of the specific family member who experienced such misfortune is unknown. Such a horrific death is the kind of thing ghostly stories and legends are made of. Katie Cox, the family member who shared this story, said the family members were divided as to whether the house was indeed haunted. Of the seven children, four believed in ghosts, while the other three did not.

Friends of the children were convinced it was indeed haunted. After spending a night in the house, they would go home and tell their parents things they had seen and heard. These children told of how they would hear the organ playing when no one was in the room. When these friends would spend the night, they would hear someone rapping on the door, but no one was there. Another friend talked about a man who could be seen walking the farm and calling out for the boys, "Come on!" just as Katie's boys had claimed. When two of Homer Manfull's girls (Lydia's granddaughters) spent the night, they claimed to have heard "hurdy-gurdy" and were so scared they ran to a neighbor's house. It is unclear whether this meant a slang term in which they heard unexplained loud noises or whether they indeed heard the instrument called a hurdy-gurdy. The instrument, when played, sounds like a violin.

After the Cox family, the house never seemed to have anyone live there for any great length of time. It was while the house sat empty during the 1930s that vandals stole or destroyed all the beautiful work Hunter had put into the house. The beautiful wood was removed, and someone ripped out the plumbing, stole the beautiful carpets and chandeliers, stripped plaster from the walls, and smashed the windows. Some believe the vandals stole what they could for money since this was during the Great Depression. When it was purchased by William E. Hibbets of Minerva in the 1950s, he did his best to restore the house. He was unable to complete many repairs, as he passed away unexpectedly due to a heart attack in 1957.

The charred remains of a once beautiful mansion that held so much mystery, 1969. *Velma Griffin collection, courtesy the Carroll County Genealogical Society.*

Several others would come to own the house and try to restore it, without luck. By the late 1960s, it had become a hangout for drifters and others who hoped to catch a glimpse of one of the ghosts. The sheriff's department stayed busy chasing them off. Around 6:00 a.m. on Saturday, April 12, 1969, the Augusta Fire Department received the call that the house was engulfed in flames. By the time the fire department arrived, the only remnants were the bricks that came from the land. The fire chief suspected that the house had been burning since just after midnight. William Cox, a grandson of Isaac and Lydia, purchased the remaining shell and three and a half acres surrounding the house and tried without avail to find someone to purchase the house and rebuild it. David Frase finally purchased the shell and the land, but instead of rebuilding, he razed the shell and built a new home on the land. The only trace of this once magnificent home is the few pieces of sandstone that served as a foundation—a sad end to a magnificent home with so much history.

CHAPTER 7

BUTLER AVENUE

Penny and her daughter were walking home from the Circle K one evening. As they walked along Butler Avenue and neared the Ashton House Museum, they heard screams. They stopped to look around and were unable to discern where the screams were coming from. As they began walking again, they heard heavy breathing, breathing so close it sounded like it was directly behind them. Quickening their pace, they continued toward their home, and just as suddenly as the other two noises had happened, a very low and menacing growl echoed out of the shadows. They did not stay to find out where the noises were coming from.

Butler Avenue is a very short street and was named for the family who once owned the land. Along this tiny street are eight houses, one museum, and an apartment building. When people first began buying land and settling in what is now Carrollton, this was all farmland. The village of Carrollton was laid out just one street over. The earliest known owner of the farm was George Gambert, who purchased the farm in 1877. Gambert married the widowed Lavinia Hawk Kintner on March 5, 1893. Just a few months later, on December 29, 1893, George sold the farm to Joseph C. Butler. George and Lavinia kept the small corner lot where their house sat. They never had children of their own, but Lavinia had four with Benjamin Kintner. One son died in infancy; their son Willard moved to Iowa; their daughter Irene married Frank Harsh in 1892; and the other daughter, Etta, married Elmer Brooks in 1893. George and Lavinia lived in the house on their corner until they were separated by George's death.

Butler Avenue looking north. Once a farm owned by Joseph C. Butler, it is now the site of several houses and a museum. *Janice Lane collection.*

According to several newspaper reports from May 1897, their home caught fire and the roof caved in on George. Lavinia was also burned, but not as badly. George was taken to Dr. Everhart's in New Harrisburg, where he could be watched hourly, but "not-withstanding the nursing and dressing of his deep scalp and body burns," Gambert died, leaving Lavinia a widow once again. One year later, she married Washington Borland, who was also widowed. Things become a bit confusing at this point. Records and family state that Washington and Lavinia moved toward Dellroy, and his obituary says he died in 1904; however, when Lavinia's mother passed away in October 1908, her obituary stated, "Died Friday morning at the home of her daughter, Mrs. Lavinia Borland, corner of High and Grant Streets." This indicates that Lavinia was still living in the home she had shared with George Gambert. By the 1910 census, Lavinia was still living on Grant Street but was now married to Cyrus Kirby.

It was also in 1910 that Joseph Butler created a subdivision now known as the Butler J.C. addition. He had the farm surveyed out, and the lots were sold off and a new street was formed. The street was named Butler Avenue.

The Butler family was well known in Carrollton. Joseph was a furniture salesman and the town undertaker. He and his wife, Cora Ebersole, lived where the Ashton House Museum now stands. According to an article in the *Free Press Standard* dated December 26, 1929, Joseph's grandfather was the first Butler to come to Carrollton. George Butler moved to Carrollton from Cumberland, Maryland, and started a tannery. He also served as a postmaster. His son Washington Butler was born in Carrollton in 1819, thirteen years before the county was formed. His obituary says that he was the oldest native-born male at the time of his death. Washington Butler had continued his father's tannery, which, according to an 1874 map, shows it was located on what is now the corner of High and Fifth Streets. Fifth Street was called Grant Street originally, meaning Lavinia's home was once part of the bigger Butler farm.

In December 1929, a news article in the paper announced a seventy-fifth birthday party for Joseph. It was held at his sister Marsha Aller's home. The article lists the other friends and family members in attendance, and there is listed another sister, Mary Aller. It just so happened that two of his sisters coincidentally married into the Aller family. Jane Marshall, as we know, was married to George Hershel, but now we learn that their sister Mary Florence married George's brother Absalom. How convenient to have an undertaker for a brother-in-law when you have a cemetery on your farm.

The couple seated in the middle of the photo are Washington Borland and his second wife, Lavinia Hawk Kintner Gambert. The photo was taken just prior to his death and her marriage to husband number four. *Courtesy Rick Borland.*

The happy Butler family would experience heartache in the home when Cora, who had been struggling with failing health for three years, suffered a stroke on March 26, 1923. She suffered for only a couple of hours before death overcame her. The family held her funeral service the following Thursday in their home. Her body was later taken to the mausoleum at Grandview Cemetery.

Joseph Butler passed away in the very same house sixteen years later. It was the same house where he was born—the Butler family farmhouse. His undertaking and furniture business was bought by W.M. Sweeney, who then conducted Butler's funeral services also in the Butler family farmhouse.

Joseph Butler was very particular when he sold off the lots he had created. The deed for the corner lot where the apartment building is now was sold to Park Beatty in 1919 and states, "No building other than a dwelling house or residence shall be erected or moved upon the premises herein conveyed." And while it has mainly been used as an apartment building, there was a time when part of it was used for offices.

A previous tenant who had an office in the building thought it might have been a theater at one time because of the way the floor sloped in one area. No evidence of that has ever been found, and it would have strictly gone against Butler's wishes. As far as records show, it was only ever used as apartments and offices. The current building was built by Park Beatty in 1920, just three years before he would build a theater in the building now known as the Virginia. This lot marks the southeastern corner of the original Butler farm.

Once called the Sloan Apartments, this apartment building seems to be the hub of activity for Butler Avenue. *Janice Lane collection.*

A local medium said that they had lived in one of the apartments at one time and had encountered "several women and a man 'living' there." Other folks who had either lived in the building or had a business in it at one time would not confirm or deny the presence of any beings in the building. All they would say was, "Yes, I've experienced strange things there."

The southwestern corner of the farm sits adjacent to what was the Hardesty Mill, which was owned by Absalom Karn's son-in-law. That corner is the present-day site of Crossroads Pizza. The current owner says he has spent a lot of time in the building and never seen or heard anything strange or ghostlike, but tenants of the apartment have complained to him of hearing strange noises at night. Former employees also claim the building is haunted but only because they have heard unexplained noises. This would seem to be common for a building occupied by multiple occupants. Other than the noises, no one has seen anything at this location.

Yet there seems to be something odd about this land that was once all one farm. Absalom Karn's son-in-law owns the property to the west; two of the Aller family married into the Butler family and were practically neighbors; and Lavinia Hawk, widow of Christian Kintner, lived on the farm. Other than this strange connection of families by marriage, there seemed to be nothing else that connected these hauntings. Again, more questions than answers have arisen. Was Lavinia a black widow? Or did she seriously just have bad luck in keeping husbands alive? And who are the women and man "living" in the apartments still? Is Joseph Butler mad because the apartments were used for offices? And just what made all those weird noises that caused Penny and her daughter to run home? Are the ghosts connected to a particular building or just the "farm" itself?

CHAPTER 8

THE VIRGINIA

If you ask any local in Carrollton for directions to the Virginia Restaurant and Lounge, they will gladly guide you. Considered a true icon in the town, the Virginia Restaurant holds the distinction of being the oldest and longest-running eatery in the area. Notably, it is also the second-oldest brick building that remains standing in the downtown area. Situated on the corner of Main Street and Municipal Parking, the building exudes a sense of history and intrigue. Given its challenging early days, it is truly remarkable that the restaurant is still thriving today.

I had the opportunity to interview Jennifer Kaser, the current owner, about her experiences in the building. As we sat at the counter eating lunch, she smiled and said that there were two distinct ghosts living in the building. One was former owner Ralph Bishop, and the other was a former part-time bartender known as Sarge. Both men passed away while staying in rooms in the upstairs hotel portion of the building.

Ralph and his wife, Birdye, ran the hotel and theater for nearly twenty years. At some point, Ralph and Birdye divorced, and he married Anna Rose. Ralph and Anna then ran the businesses until his death in 1954. Anna married James Powell, and the Powells continued operating it until 1960. Ralph Bishop had an interesting background. The Virginia seemed to be the only stable thing in his life. At nineteen, Ralph went off to fight in World War I, leaving behind a bride and infant daughter. Upon his return, he reunited with them only to have her leave in 1923. He then married Birdye, who was herself a divorced war bride with a small child.

A current view of the Virginia Restaurant and Lounge, the longest-running restaurant in Carrollton. *Janice Lane collection.*

The lobby of then Park Theater taken around 1923. Notice the strange lights in the doorway just under the word "Little." Some ghosts may be older than originally thought. *Courtesy Carroll County Genealogical Society.*

Now part of the Virginia Lounge, this stage is what remains of the theater. It is also the site where Sarge has been seen still keeping an eye on the place. *Janice Lane collection.*

As mentioned earlier, Ralph and Birdye divorced, and he then married Anna Rose. Yet, somehow Ralph died all alone in a hotel room and was then buried several counties away beside his stepdaughter. Perhaps he stays at the Virginia because it was the only place that truly felt like home to him. One wonders how he feels about sharing this space with Sarge.

Sarge's real name was Larry Snodgrass. Larry was a dedicated employee at the Virginia Bar and Lounge since its opening in 1988. His responsibility was to make sure everything was in place for the evening. He sometimes tended the bar and served as a bouncer. Following his passing, multiple witnesses have reported sightings of Sarge lingering in the establishment, either standing at the bar or strolling across the stage. He is easily recognizable by his signature red shirt, a garment he was often seen wearing during his time at the bar.

One evening, a couple was visiting the bar when the woman decided to use the ladies' room in the basement. Soon after, she hurriedly returned to her companion and urged him to leave immediately. Concerned, Jennifer Kaser asked what had happened, and the lady recounted her unsettling experience. While she was using the facilities, someone began knocking on all the stall doors. Despite looking around, the woman did not see anyone

62

else present. Jennifer could not help but suspect that it might have been Sarge, the lingering presence in the bar.

Jennifer also shared that her ex-husband had been skeptical about her stories regarding Sarge and Ralph until he had his own experience. One day, he was working in the men's room near the lounge with a friend. As the friend stepped out of the room for a brief moment, Jennifer's ex-husband noticed someone ascending the flight of stairs beside him. Assuming it was his friend, he called out to them. To his surprise, there was no response. Puzzled, he approached the stairs and called out again, only to hear his friend's voice responding from behind him. This eerie encounter left him with no choice but to acknowledge that something strange was happening in the building.

She also recounted a story that the building's previous owner had shared with her. During the 1970s, the rooms were rented out to couples while the husbands worked on gas and oil lines. One couple made a strange request, asking that a picture of a woman sitting at a piano be removed from their room. They claimed that the woman in the picture would come and sit on the edge of their bed in the middle of the night, making them quite nervous. Without hesitation, the hotel owner moved the picture to another room. However, several weeks later, another couple who were staying in the room where the picture had been moved made the same request. They claimed that the same woman was standing at the foot of their bed in the middle of the night, leaving them feeling terrified. Convinced that something was not right about the picture, the owner decided to get rid of it altogether.

While Jennifer was sharing these stories with me, our waitress laughed and said we were both crazy. She had been working at the Virginia for quite some time and had never seen or heard anything strange. Jennifer and I both shrugged, and Jennifer teased that maybe the ghosts just did not like her. We continued talking and discussed how the building had gone through a lot of changes over the years, the biggest being the remodeling after two fires. Jennifer said that after the second fire, everything had been completely fireproofed. The doors, walls, everything had been made of a metal that would not burn. Because of this, when a third fire broke out, it was contained to one room. Someone died in that fire, but to the best of her knowledge, that person was not still staying there. A few seconds later, the waitress asked if we smelled smoke and asked the cook what she was burning.

The cook replied that she was not burning anything. Jennifer got up and went to stand in the doorway between the kitchen and the basement and agreed that she, too, smelled smoke. Curiosity got the better of me, and I went to sniff for myself and smelled it too. Only, it did not smell like burning food or wood but more like cigar smoke. Another server came over, and she could smell it too. So, Jennifer went to the basement to investigate and found nothing. She then went upstairs and, again, nothing. The server yelled at us that we had stirred something up and now our ghosts were messing with her.

As previously mentioned, the building had a recurring problem with fires. It was evident from the very start that this would be a concern. Shortly after acquiring the land in 1829, William Jenkins began constructing the brick structure that is still in use to this day. On January 1, 1830, the first fire occurred. This did not stop Jenkins. He immediately cleared out the burned wood and opened his store on January 2, 1830. He took out insurance but failed to pay for it. The building was repossessed by the insurance company and sold in 1846 to Edward Lukens. It would later be sold to Enos Hoopes and be called Hoopes House. Hoopes was also the superintendent of the county infirmary. He ran the hotel until 1891, when his son, W.S. Hoopes, took over. Then, Daisy Whitcraft ran it for a while. Around 1923, it was called the Colonial House and closed for a brief time while Park Beatty added a theater. Park Beatty sold it to George Bundy, and the name was changed to the Central Hotel. Around 1935, Ralph Bishop purchased the building and is recorded as having been the person to fireproof the building after another devastating fire in 1936. Perhaps this is his reason for staying and protecting the building and why the smell of smoke often follows him. Ralph also renamed the theater and restaurant the Virginia.

Ghosts apparently like Jennifer, which seems to be a good thing. In late 2023, Jennifer was busy hanging curtains she had just washed. Unable to place a ladder in front of the window, she was standing on the seat of the booth putting the curtains onto the rod when she distinctly heard the heavy metal door between the restaurant and the hallway to the lounge open and close. This door is locked with a deadbolt and not something that could easily open and close by itself. All the other staff had gone home, and Jennifer was alone in the building.

She went to investigate and found the door was indeed closed and locked. Used to the pranks of her ghosts, she went back to hanging the curtains. Standing on the seat once again, she started hearing strange noises. First there was scratching, as if something was in the walls. Then she heard water running. This was followed by a knocking. Jennifer said she looked up, and that's when she saw the ceiling rise up and then come back down. As it started to do it again, she ran toward the kitchen. She was about halfway across the room when she turned and saw the entire ceiling coming down,

The Park Theater stage taken around 1923 when the theater opened. *Courtesy Isaac Brumm and Jay Stoneman.*

almost as if it was being peeled away. She made it to the kitchen just as the entire ceiling collapsed. Call it coincidence if you like, but some of us believe that one of the ghosts opened and closed that back door and made all those noises to save her from a nasty injury or worse. Jennifer thanked the ghosts for saving her life.

Soon after that, a group of ghost hunters came to the restaurant and did an investigation. They told Jennifer there are at least seven different entities living in the building. Only two have been identified, Ralph and Sarge. It is unlikely that the other five will ever be identified. As long as they keep helping and do not cause harm, Jennifer is content to let the ghosts stay. She also has a ghost at her home just a few blocks away. She has seen a white-haired lady in the yard on several occasions.

CHAPTER 9

THE TAYLOR / BOYLAN FARM

L et's face it, any basement that is dark, damp, and has a dirt floor is scary, but one with tales of people being buried in it is worse. Mikki Timberlake shared the story of her grandparents' farm. Rumors claim that an owner of the house came home and found his wife having an affair. He then killed his wife and her lover and buried them in the dirt floor under the stairs. After that, anyone who used the stairs claimed they could feel someone grab their ankles from behind. If something sinister happened in the house, there is no record of it. The power of suggestion may have caused people to think something was reaching through the stairs and grabbing at them. Dirt floors in centuries-old houses often create a spookiness that can make the mind see or sense things.

While no evidence was found to corroborate the story of a man killing his wife in the house, something possibly darker was discovered. It was learned that this 160-acre farm may have been part of an old Native American burial ground. According to an archaeological atlas made by Fred J. Heer in 1912, there were a few sites around Carrollton that were once used by the Native Americans. Less than a mile from the Taylor farm was a site Heer marked as an Indian village. There were two other sites marked that indicated burial sites or hunting grounds. These were just the ones he knew of. Other research and maps show that Natives used more than the three sites marked by Heer. Sites in Union Township and around Leesville were most commonly known. As late as 1820, most of northwestern Ohio was considered Indian land, and that territory covered most of what was then

A modern photo of the Taylor/Boylan house, where reports of something grabbing ankles in the basement have occurred. *Courtesy Mikki Timberlake.*

Tuscarawas County and included the portion that would become Carroll County. It is nearly impossible to prove or locate the exact location of these sites in today's day and age.

So, if the farm was indeed on a Native American burial ground, what does that mean? Lore over the centuries has always said that Native American burial grounds are extremely sacred. Disturbing them in any way is dangerous on multiple levels. Bad things always happen to anyone who disturbs this sacred ground. Other tales and lore about the Native Americans in this area only fuel these stories.

Early settlers who lived along a nearby creek would complain of seeing a "devilish" apparition. The Native American legend called it a "wendigo." The definition of this creature was a cannibalistic monster that was often associated with winter that would stalk and eat humans or possess a human and turn them into a monstrous killer. It takes a lot of faith and imagination to think this would be what was causing hauntings on the Taylor farm. However, it is quite odd that at least two men who committed murder had a connection to the property.

One was a next-door neighbor to the Taylor farm. Mr. Kertes was convicted of robbing and killing Hi Berlin in 1942. Not too far away was the site of another gruesome killing involving an estranged husband and the owner of the Carroll House Truck Stop. The Taylor farm, the Kertes home, and the truck stop were all within a mile of the Native American burial ground. So, when these men committed these crimes and claimed, "The devil made me do it," perhaps it was not the devil but something every bit as dark and sinister. Those stories will be saved for another time.

So, did John George Taylor build his home on a burial ground? Possibly. Or perhaps just close enough that he brought trouble to his family. Of course, the older the home, the more tales there seem to be of ghosts inhabiting it. This particular farm that once belonged to John George Taylor in Harrison Township is no exception. He was born in Troy, New York, in 1821. He moved to Augusta, Ohio, with his parents and siblings around the age of seven, and according to U.S. military records, he became a West Point cadet after his high school graduation in 1838. On June 1, 1843, he married Nancy Lewton, and in 1847, they moved to Illinois. They lived there for four years before returning to Carroll County and purchasing the 160 acres just three miles outside Carrollton. John would return to military service on November 5, 1862. He enlisted in Company G, 125th Ohio, during the Civil War and served as a sergeant with the Union army. No records say why, but he was discharged in July 1863 and returned home to his wife and twelve children.

Both the *Carroll Chronicle* and the *Free Press* posted obituaries for Taylor saying he died of "creeping paralysis." He was buried in Baxter's Ridge Cemetery just a short distance from his home. His father, Robert Taylor, is also buried in Baxter's Ridge Cemetery, having been buried there after dying on his son's farm nearby. Both men were well respected in the area. John Taylor was said to have been an honest man who worked hard his whole life. During his years in Carroll County, he served as a township trustee and clerk. For a time, he was elected as the director of the local infirmary. Apparently, he was a very respected man who was not likely to have killed his wife.

After his death, his daughter Mary Etta and her husband, Thomas Jefferson Riegle, became the new owners of the house and farm. This was also an unlikely thing to have happen if your father had killed your mother. Maybe it was Riegle who had a dark side. Or maybe he became overwhelmed with depression at the loss of his wife.

Thomas and Mary Etta and their nine children would live in the house for only a short time. They took possession of the house in 1902, and Mary Etta died in 1907, just six months after the birth of their youngest son, Wilber. The cause of her death was not found. Six months after her death, Wilber, who had just turned a year old, also suddenly died. Thomas Riegle would marry two more times and then was buried with all three wives and two of his sons, Wilber and John T., at Grandview Cemetery. John T. Riegle had moved to Pittsburgh after marrying Esther Heck. He worked as an electrician for a steel plant. His marriage announcement in the *Free Press* on June 30, 1910, tells of his marriage and says, "Mr. and Mrs. Reigle [*sic*] are spending a couple weeks in the home of his parents, Mr. and Mrs. T.J. Reigle, near New Harrisburg." This would have been his dad and stepmom, Mary Frances. This indicates the Riegle family was still living on the Taylor farm in 1910, although Mary Etta's and Wilber's deaths in 1907 supposedly happened in Harlem Springs. In tax records, Thomas is still listed as the landowner in 1915. This raises the question of why Mary Etta and Wilber were not living at home at the time of their deaths. It is quite possible that Mary Etta and Wilber were both suffering from some disease that took them to Harlem Springs. It was known for its natural springs that were said to have healing properties and had a resort that many famous people are said to have visited. All this proves is that Mary Etta died by a known cause and not by the hand of a scorned husband. None of this explains the tale of bodies buried in the basement.

Let's rewind a bit. Like all of Carroll County, the land was originally part of the Northwest Territory. In 1806, just three years after Ohio became a state, a group of brothers came from Maryland by way of Pennsylvania and purchased land from the Steubenville Land Office. Jesse, Sutton Jr., Nathan, and John Leggett all purchased several acres of what is now Carroll County. Jesse's portion was the property in question. Jesse also brought his wife, Mary, and six of their children to this new land. After the couple settled on the farm, four more children were born. Jesse acquired additional acreage in 1824. In 1844, he was named in a lawsuit in which George Leggett's widow was suing because she needed money to pay off her deceased husband's debts. Along with Jesse were the names of Mrs. Leggett's father, two of her brothers, Samuel Harsh, Nancy Taylor, William Taylor, Patterson Taylor, and Sally Taylor. Yet no connection could be made between the families other than this lawsuit.

Jesse Leggett sold his farm in 1855 to John Taylor and moved to Iowa. Again, there is no connection to any murders. We know that John Taylor's daughter and her husband were the next owners, but what about the family after them? The next owner was Wallace Boylan. Wallace and his wife, Belle, purchased the farm in 1920 and leased the farm to Franklin Ellsworth Campbell. Campbell and his wife, Ada, did not live in the house;

This was the house built by the Taylor family, pictured here in 1966 while it belonged to the Boylan family. *Courtesy Mikki Timberlake.*

they only worked the farmland. Their home was actually in Carrollton on the corner of High and Second Streets. Yes, the corner facing the Butler farm. This seems like a very strange coincidence, but that still does not explain the story.

Wallace and Belle's son John inherited the property, and it was his family that was first told that there were bodies buried in the basement. Maybe someone was just trying to scare them. Or maybe there is something "living" in the basement of this house. Is something grabbing ankles, or is it imagination? The current owners feel that the cellar does have a creepiness factor, but they have not experienced anything—yet.

CHAPTER 10

MORGES, THE WORLEY INN, AND ZION CEMETERY

You would be hard-pressed to find it on a map, but in 1840, the village of Morges (pronounced "MOR-jez") was said to have a population of 1,593. Some argue that it was never that big. With over five hundred burials in its cemetery, perhaps it did have a larger population decades ago. It was originally called Moregg and was settled when Akey Worley built a hotel and tavern there in 1820 as a stagecoach stop. He brought his family to the area shortly after the War of 1812, when the land was part of Stark County. It was the halfway point between Bolivar and Canton and was on the main stagecoach route between Canton, Bolivar, and Steubenville. Farmers would haul their wheat to Bolivar via this route. As it was a halfway point, many would stop here for the night. The village once had the Griffith Hotel and Tavern; a saloon owned by Sealy Madden, who it is said did her own bouncing when patrons became unruly; a drugstore; a wagoner's shop; four blacksmiths; and an iron ore pit. Today, it has a few houses, a church, and a cemetery located at the crossroads of two country roads. When stagecoaches became a thing of the past, so did the population of Morges. Now it is considered part of Magnolia, Ohio, and its population is unknown.

While the stagecoaches were popular, the taverns were too. Worley's tavern sat where St. Mary's parking lot is today. The inn was a vibrant and thriving establishment in the 1820s with a sinister story. The tavern was torn down in 1923, but former residents remembered playing in the building as children. One of those former residents, Adam Burwell, left a letter that talked about the old village. He recalled playing in the inn as a child:

That old tavern was still standing when I was a kid. It had a closet or dungeon as it was called at that time. It had a trap door but no steps. Quite all of the pack peddlers who stopped there disappeared forever. I played hide and seek with the other boys and often we would drop down into it. There were quite a few bones on the bottom and they were human bones. I will not mention any of the names of the folks who operated it at that time, but I know, through granddad's diary, of course. The farmers were not robbed as they had their teams and if they had not arrived home, they would have been looked after, but the peddlers were all strangers and not missed.

Burwell told how the lady who ran the tavern would seat the lonely peddlers at a table near a curtain at dinnertime. When no one was watching, her son would hit the victim on the back of the head, drag him through the curtain, steal any belongings, and then throw him into the pit. Mother and son were finally caught, and the Tuscarawas County sheriff sent them to prison for life.

News articles from that time show that Burwell's memory was a little off. Mrs. Athey did indeed run a boardinghouse, but she did not have a son and especially not one old enough to help in the crimes. She was convicted of murder after bodies were found in her basement and was sentenced to life in the state penitentiary.

Whether it was the Atheys, the Worleys, or someone else, stories of the stagecoach murders at that inn and others nearby were unfortunately very common. Although the building and its basement have long faded away, strange noises and apparitions wandering the nearby cemetery have been reported. One apparition that was commonly reported was of an old peddler wandering through the cemetery on a moonlit night still carrying his pack on his back. Could he be one of Athey's victims?

St. Mary's of the Immaculate Conception Catholic Church seems to be what keeps this tiny "town" alive. The church was built in 1851 with bricks burned on the property. The adjoining cemetery is even older. The first burial found among the standing stones is that of Catherine Zengler in 1830. Records claim there were two other burials in 1830: that of John Little, the fifteen-year-old son of Mathias Little, and eighteen-year-old Catherine Renier, the daughter of Stephen Renier. However, no tombstones have been found for them nor any records.

The congregation first began in the home of the town's co-founder, John Waggoner. Soon after, a wooden chapel was built, and it was called St. Tidelis of Sigmaringen. Members met in the wooden chapel until it burned

Left: St. Mary's of the Immaculate Conception Church in Morges, Ohio. *Courtesy Enna Lame Photography.*

Below: St. Mary's of the Immaculate Conception Church, cemetery, and rectory in Morges, Ohio. *Janice Lane collection.*

in 1849. In need of a place to worship, they built the brick building and renamed their congregation St. Mary's. The rectory was built in 1853, also from bricks made on the property. Waggoner, who donated the ground where the church now sits, was buried near the church in 1871 after suffering from a fall while trying to help repair the church roof. Some claim he is buried right where he fell.

In 1905, Father Louis Mandery was assigned as the resident priest. He served the church until his death in 1948, the longest-serving priest in the church's history. At one time, Father Mandery heard strange noises coming from the cemetery. He went to investigate and caught some men trying to remove a porcelain image from a grave. At that time, he was able to scare them off, but at some point, someone succeeded in removing the image. The grave was that of Peter Ross. At the bottom of the stone is engraved, "Killed by the Italian Black Hand." Vandals tried to scratch this off but were unable to succeed.

Gravestone of Peter Ross. The circle in the middle once held a porcelain image of Ross, and you can see where someone tried to destroy the wording "Black Hand" on the bottom. *Courtesy Jon Papai.*

Why was Ross's grave so intriguing? News articles of his death hit nearly every Ohio newspaper in 1925. He had been out for a drive with his wife, his brother, and his brother-in-law. Upon returning home, they drove up to the garage. Mrs. Ross and Mr. Ross's brother headed for the house while the brother-in-law went to open the garage door. Shots came out of nowhere. Peter was shot twice, and the fatal shot was the one in his heart. There was a lot of confusion, and no one seemed to see the shooter. It was believed the gunman disappeared into the nearby woods. Mrs. Ross told authorities that she had no idea why someone would want to kill her husband.

Peter Ross had been a foreman for the National Fireproofing plant near Magnolia, Ohio. The *Daily Times* of New Philadelphia, Ohio, made it clear that Ross was an Italian and that the Canton Italian band had aided in the funeral rites. In their book *Ohio's Black Hand Syndicate: The Birth of Organized Crime in America*, David Meyers and Elise Meyers Walker explain how the terms "mafia" and "black hand" were synonymous for a secret society of loosely organized Italian criminals. We have all heard the stories of the mob and gangsters in America; we just never realized they were right here in small-town Ohio. Apparently, someone thought Ross's death was connected to the Black Hand since it was engraved on his stone. There are not many homes in Morges, so it was not likely to have been a robbery gone wrong, and the shooter seemed to have lain in wait for Ross to return home. This was impressive shooting to have supposedly been hiding in the nearby woods and hit Ross in the heart through a car door. Since it has been nearly one hundred years and his death was never solved, perhaps Peter is still wandering the Morges cemetery.

If the ghost is Mr. Ross, he and the pack peddler are not alone. The most disturbing ghost reported is that of a headless little girl, about four years of age. No one knows who she may be. She is reportedly dressed in 1880s clothing and simply wanders the cemetery. A report states that an old tombstone says, "She died mysteriously." This stone was not located, and those of young children that were located say they all died from accidents and illness.

Not all the ghosts stayed in the cemetery; ghosts seem to have taken up residency in the church rectory as well. A rectory is a house designated for a priest. The St. Mary's rectory sits adjacent to the church and the cemetery. Just inside the back door of the rectory are the stairs to the second floor. This stairway is one of those steep, narrow flights of stairs common in many old houses where the turn at the bottom is very tight and dangerous. One apparition that was seen on more than one occasion was that of an adult figure that seemed to have no form. A Catholic surplice (the white robe-type garment worn during services by priests) could be seen entering the house from the cemetery and then going up those steep stairs. Then noises were heard upstairs, as if someone were moving things around.

A visiting missionary was staying in the bedroom upstairs, and he reported back to the Steubenville Diocese that he awoke to the sound of "a thousand hissing snakes." He grabbed his clothes, fled downstairs, dressed, and relocated to a local hotel. There he spent the rest of the night praying.

Father Karjovick served the church and lived in the rectory for one year in 1966. He, too, had heard and seen things in the cemetery and in his home, one of them being the bodiless surplice. One night as he prepared for bed, a black snake slithered across his upstairs bedroom floor. He became convinced that it was something evil that possessed his house and not the spirits of past parishioners. He appealed to the Steubenville Diocese, and the bishop sent a priest to investigate.

The investigating priest encountered things like a rocking chair that would rock itself to the point of nearly tipping over. This was followed by distinct,

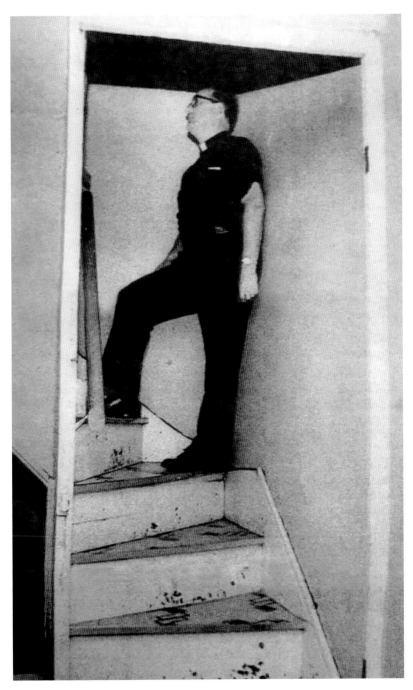

Father Clair Dinger is showing the staircase in the St. Mary's Rectory where ghosts were heard coming and going. *The Velma Griffin collection, courtesy Carroll County Genealogical Society.*

unexplained banging in the basement, night and day. The noise was so pronounced that the plumbers who were called in to find a problem refused to stay in the house alone. The priest also became frustrated with a back door that would open and close on its own. On more than one occasion, the door would shut and lock the priest out.

Father Paul Richter, an expert on the rite of exorcism, was then sent to the rectory. He concluded that there was nothing there and left. In preparation for sending Father Richter, the bishop had requested information on the church. It was learned that attendance had dwindled to fewer than a dozen attendees. Both the bishop and Father Richter felt that Father Karjovick was simply trying to gain attention and thus increase attendance. Father Karjovick was frustrated that no one believed him and that no one was coming to his aid, so he took it upon himself to perform the exorcism. He blessed water and sprinkled it throughout the rectory and the church, and unbeknownst to his parishioners, he drove to their homes and sprinkled it in their yards. At each home, he prayed that the evil spirits would leave and people would return to the church. That was in December, and by the Christmas Eve service, so many people turned up for confession that the priest had to have his meal delivered to the church.

In 1973, Father Dinger was assigned to the church. Upon hearing the stories of what Father Karjovick had experienced, he spent the first few nights on the couch. Once he was brave enough to go up to the bedroom, he left the lights on. Although he never saw any apparitions, he did hear things he could not explain. Most of the noises were explained as the house settling; however, the rectory was built with bricks that are stacked, so the walls are a foot thick. It is unlikely he heard the one-hundred-plus-year-old house settling. He claimed the exorcism of his predecessor must have worked.

Another legend is that of a hunting party in the woods near the cemetery. The men were out coon hunting when their dogs frantically ran to the base of a tree and barked and lunged at whatever they had caught. The men caught up to the dogs and discovered they had treed something in a pine on the edge of the cemetery. Lifting their lantern to look for the glint of light in a coon's eyes, one of the men fell back, startled. Instead of a racoon, he saw the figure of his dear friend who had died five years earlier. One of the other men looked and saw nothing. Still, the dogs had to be dragged from the tree.

While some claim ghosts will not haunt a cemetery, there are plenty of others who will tell you of their spooky experiences in a cemetery. A group with an electronic voice phenomenon (EVP) recorder was at the Augusta

Christian Church cemetery testing out their equipment. They knew no one buried there and were randomly reading off names. They passed a gravestone, and one of the men said, "There's Ken." Very distinctly through the EVP they heard, "Kenneth." The gentleman whose grave they had passed was adamant during his living years that his name was Kenneth, not Ken or Kenny.

A lesser-known haunted cemetery is Zion Cemetery in Sherrodsville, Ohio. When Samuel and Artlisa Davis married in 1878, they had hopes and dreams of a peaceful life, just like everyone else. There was no way they could foresee the tragedies yet to befall them. The winter of 1892 was hard for a lot of people. The world was gripped by an influenza pandemic much like the one we suffered through in 2020. The Davis family was no exception. Their son John T. Davis was a week shy of his fifth birthday when diphtheria took his life. His baby sister Birtha Mae was only a year and a half old when she died nineteen days later. Still reeling from this loss, Samuel and Artlisa had another child named Ola on July 4, 1894. Records do not indicate what happened to poor Ola, but she lived for only nineteen days and then she, too, was buried next to her brother and sister.

Distraught over the loss, the parents had a special memorial created for their children. Samuel worked with the local funeral home, and it is believed

The Davis children's gravestone. Notice how the eyes seem to be glaring at you. *Janice Lane collection.*

that he may have carved the stone himself. Whether he carved it or hired someone, it has been the topic of many who have visited the Zion Cemetery.

Some call it hauntingly beautiful. Others find it disturbing. The grave marker was carved from a single piece of sandstone. The carver supposedly used images of the two older children to create the work. Descendants of the family say the resemblance to other family members is remarkable. The stone also includes carvings of a snake sneaking up on a bird in her nest and a rabbit hiding behind rocks and ferns. There is also an anchor with a broken rope. These have also caused much debate. Some believe they were carved to symbolize the untimely loss of the children. The rabbit represents young life and innocence, and the snake was meant to represent eternal life, as a snake sheds its skin and perpetuates new life. This was to mean the children had shed their earthly lives for heavenly ones. The snake attacking the nest also represented the children being snatched from life too soon. The anchor with a broken rope shows how they were no longer tethered to the earth.

A former funeral home director who had known Samuel Davis said the father had indeed carved the stone. The father carved the animals because they were simply ones loved by his children. It may have been both. Either way, it is indeed intricately carved and has held up well for its age and despite the attacks of vandals over the years. Vandals became such a problem that in 1980, someone thought it would preserve the stone if it were covered with aluminum paint. This paint unfortunately covered many of the facial details of the children and destroyed the stone's integrity. It also created another problem: passersby would claim to see a ghost running through the cemetery. The sheriff was asked to investigate, and he determined that this ghost appeared only in the winter months when there were no leaves on the trees and the aluminum paint was reflecting lights from Atwood Lodge.

There are some who refuse to believe the sheriff's explanation, as they say they have seen the ghostly shadow in other times of the year. A post on the Haunted Ohio Facebook page shared that in the late 1990s, a group was walking through the Zion Cemetery, and even though it had not rained in days, they saw tears running down the face of one of the children. This is not something that would have been caused by lights reflecting off aluminum paint.

There are no other family members buried with the children. This topic has caused some debate as well. What happened to the parents? Why are they not buried with their children? It is believed that the pain was too much for Samuel and Artlisa, and they moved away to try to move on with their

The Davis children keep watch over the Zion Cemetery. *Janice Lane collection.*

lives. They had three other children to think of as well. Artlisa died in Akron but is buried in Kilgore, Ohio. As of the writing of this work, it is unknown what happened to Samuel. He died before 1910, as Artlisa is listed as a widow in the 1910 census. Maybe the children could feel the heartbreak of their father, who likely poured sweat and tears into the stone if he did indeed carve it. So, maybe the children are still there, searching for their parents, who are buried elsewhere.

CHAPTER 11

THE HOUSE ON MAIN STREET

The family was sitting at the dining room table playing a game, and mom had a green metal planter set off to the side. Suddenly, the planter began to rock, slid off the table, stayed in midair for a few seconds, and then fell to the floor. No one spoke for twenty minutes." That is how the story of the next house begins. The home served as a rental property for many years, and various tenants have complained of the strange happenings.

In another incident, a family friend had gone upstairs to use the bathroom and returned looking extremely pale. When the others asked her what had happened, she said she had seen someone sitting on the edge of the waterbed. In a jesting manner, their mom jokingly yelled that the ghost had better not be sitting on her bed. Later that night, as their mom went to retire to her room, she felt something slam into her chest and knock the wind out of her. She had to step back out of the room and catch her breath.

Visions of various "people" have been seen in the rooms. A young girl in a frilly white dress was once seen sitting on a box fan in one of the bedrooms. A teenage girl was seen standing beside the bed in the same room on another occasion. A man was standing and staring out a window another time. Many tenants have complained of doors opening and closing by themselves. Some say they could clearly hear their names being called by someone in another part of the house when no one else was home.

One night, the living tenants of the house were gathered in the living room watching a movie when all the lights went out. Before they could figure out what was happening, a flash of light shot through the living room and darted up the stairs. They also watched a sheer white figure pace in front of the attic windows on another occasion.

Was it the sheer white figure in the attic, the man by the bedroom window, or the girl sitting on the fan who would mess with the dishes in the china cabinet and clank items together? Whatever it was, their cat saw it too. They witnessed the cat in a full-on fight with something none of them could see. Whatever the cat was fighting was strong enough that the cat's fur was flying. That family lived in the house for eight years and experienced many strange events. Their son was so terrified that he moved out and refused to tell his mom and sister what had happened. An aunt spent the night and woke the next day with unexplained scratches on her chest. Other tenants heard noises and would catch glimpses of something moving through the house in their peripheral vision, but they never let it bother them.

The history of the land where this house now stands is quite extensive. The lot was first purchased by John Fawcett from Peter Bohart, who laid out the town of Carrollton. It would become the site of a tannery, a law office, and eventually a furniture maker's shop and home. The furniture shop was owned by Absalom Karn.

Absalom Karn was a well-known and very respected furniture maker. He had an indentured servant, an eighteen-year-old boy by the name of George Best, who disappeared in 1847. For over a month, George's legal guardian, C.F. Best, ran ads in the *Carroll Free Press* offering a ten-dollar reward for any information on the boy's whereabouts. Nothing indicates that he was ever found. This seems to be the beginning of trouble for Karn.

In 1875, Karn lost the love of his life, his beloved wife, Sarah. Her death certificate shows that she died of cancer. This was the first recorded death found for anyone who lived in the house. She died in one of the upstairs bedrooms. Sarah was the daughter of Conrad Frederick Best and Mary Anna Henneberger. Conrad Frederick was likely the C.F. Best who posted the reward for the missing George. Upon doing some more genealogy research to see how George may have been related to Sarah, it was discovered that there were no records of George other than when he was assigned to C.F. to be his ward and the multiple ads seeking his whereabouts. More interesting was the fact that Conrad Frederick's stepmom was none other than Mary Susannah Kintner. You may remember that surname. Mary Susannah was Clement Kintner's aunt. The connections become more and more intertwined, and it begins to feel as though all of the ghosts are

The former Karn home with Karn's workshop in the back. *Courtesy Enna Lame Photography.*

related. It is a small town, but even for us, this is weird. Another Kintner relative might have become a ghost. And it does not stop there.

Absalom Karn was a well-known and well-respected member of the Carrollton community. He served as borough and township treasurer for over twenty years. He was a main supplier of furniture to the Deckman store in Malvern and a prominent member of the Methodist Episcopal Church. Sometime before his wife's death, their son William and his family had moved into the small house attached to the workshop in the back of the property. Absalom was very fond of his daughter-in-law Stella and his granddaughter Valeria. They most likely moved in to help care for Sarah during her illness. William Karn was also quite well known in the community. He was a marshal for the local police department, working mostly at night, and advertisements in the local papers show he owned a successful marble business on the east side of Public Square.

It was reported by many that after Sarah's death, Absalom changed. His usually jovial demeanor was replaced by a forlorn state. His housekeeper made this statement after his death, "Like too many, after a life of abstinence, he resorted to alcoholic stimulants to nerve him against the troubles he experienced at that time of life." There was something else that made Absalom's demeanor change. Something happened that caused William and Stella to separate. Records do not indicate exactly what happened between William and his family, but they do indicate a problem. An article in the *Carroll Chronicle* from May 1879 tells us that the "Council has deemed it necessary to put Mr. Karn on duty again as Night Policeman." It continues to tell us that he was paid thirty dollars a night, and the townspeople felt it was unnecessary, since there were only a few hundred people in the town and they already had a sheriff and deputies. The tone of the article sounds as though they did not want Karn back on duty for personal reasons. Another article from 1880 tells us that Stella had filed for divorce and taken Valeria and moved to Canton. This was apparently too much for Absalom.

March 1, 1880, began like any other day. Mrs. Fisher, Absalom's live-in housekeeper, called him to breakfast at about 7:00 a.m. She would later tell authorities that Karn drank only a little coffee and was unable to keep it down. Mr. and Mrs. Fisher both worried about Absalom but decided he seemed no different than he had been most recently. Both noted that Absalom had a revolver with him as he headed out to his workshop. Absalom told them he planned to shoot rats and dogs. Soon after he went out, they heard two shots fired. This was also typical behavior for Karn. What had not been typical was the moaning and wailing he had done in his sleep the night before. That had concerned them, but they did not know what to do about it.

A neighbor, Aaron Wagner, was walking along the street that morning when he saw Absalom standing in the door of the upstairs of his furniture workshop. Wagner thought it was odd and a little dangerous for a man of Karn's age to be standing there. Karn had one hand against each side of the door and seemed to be teetering. When he saw Wagner, he turned and went back inside.

Around noon, Karn was supposed to attend a meeting with the township trustees to discuss finances since he was the treasurer. When Karn failed to appear at the meeting, Richard Runion and Elias Stonebrook went looking for him. They first searched his back workshop, then the front showroom, and finally went upstairs to the furniture storage room. They found Absalom lying on a pile of mattresses in the corner. At first, they believed him to be sleeping, possibly passed out from drinking. This was not the case.

The shots fired earlier in the morning had not been Karn shooting at rats. Stonebrook and Runion called for Dr. Stockon, who in turn solicited the help of Dr. Tripp. They confirmed that Absalom Karn was dead and called for the coroner, Dr. Skeeles. Dr. Skeeles performed a more thorough investigation and interviewed the witnesses. The accounts of Stonebrook and Runion, Mr. and Mrs. Fisher, Wagner, and both doctors were published in both local papers in full detail. Looking at the reports with today's knowledge, it seems to be too neat and tidy. Dr. Mandal Haas, current Carroll County coroner, agreed with Dr. Skeeles's findings. Dr. Haas believed that due to Karn's mental state, he likely did decide it was time to leave this earth. However, it is also possible that there was something else going on. There was no note or letter left by Karn. The position of the body might have happened from the force of the shot, but he could have been placed there as well. Other questions arose upon reading the reports.

It was unclear where the revolver had come from. Mrs. Fisher stated that she had not seen that particular gun prior to the coroner finding it. It was also not common for the average person to own such a weapon. Revolvers were typically reserved for military. Karn's son, William, had served in the Sixth Illinois Infantry during the Civil War; the gun may have been his. Another question arose about Karn's ability to be shooting rats and dogs within the village limits. Surely neighbors would have complained about this behavior. Yet it seemed to be commonplace. Maybe his son, the policeman, was giving him some leeway.

Wagner claimed to have been in front of the elementary school on Second Street Northwest watching Karn in his workroom on Main Street, which was also in the back of the house and closer to Second Street Southwest. This view is obstructed today by the house itself. There are also several other houses and buildings in the way that were confirmed to have been there in 1880. The only way Wagner could have seen Karn is if he was actually walking along Main Street.

When Karn was found, his body was lying diagonally across a stack of mattresses with only his feet hanging off the corner. Dr. Haas confirmed that the position of the body was possible if Karn had been standing or sitting on that corner. The force might have caused his body to fall back the full length of the mattresses. Dr. Haas also agreed that it was odd the only blood at the scene was a "trickle from the corner of his mouth." He was surprised to learn that there was none at the site of the entry wound. Surely there should have been some that trickled down his cheek.

Either way, Karn was gone, causing quite the uproar for this little "Burrough."

A few weeks later, it was learned that this beloved township treasurer was in debt to the township for $400; he still owed the cemetery $200 for his

A close-up of Anna Nihart Wagner. Is she still "living" in her home on Main Street? *Courtesy Richard Rainsberger.*

wife's funeral expenses; and he owed the village $937.20. It was not made clear why he owed the township and village, but as the treasurer, it might have been money he embezzled. The total amount would be over $30,000 in today's terms. What had happened to such a well-respected and trusted man to make him take that kind of money?

His home and workshop were sold at public auction to help recover the monies owed to the township. Absalom's daughter Mary Melinda Hardesty bought the property back at that auction on June 11, 1880. Mary and her husband, Frank Hardesty, lived there until 1911. This was convenient for Frank, whose gristmill was just behind the furniture store on Second Street Southwest. The mill, which he co-owned with his brother Kirk, was moved to High Street, and they sold the Main Street house to newlyweds Harry and Anna Wagner.

The Wagners and their five children would live a quiet and happy life there for several years. That is, until 1925, just ten months after the birth of their fifth child, when Anna succumbed to pneumonia. She was the third confirmed death in the house. Anna died in the same upstairs bedroom as Sarah Karn. Anna's funeral was held in the living room before she was taken to Grandview Cemetery and buried.

Harry Wagner remained in the home and raised the children alone. According to the 1950 census, his daughter Sarah and her family were living with Harry. When Harry died in 1969, Sarah and her husband sold the house to Roy and Georgette Huff. It was about this time it became a rental property. Without rental records, it is impossible to know who else lived and died there.

Karn may be the man who still stands in the window staring out into the yard. His wife, Sarah, might be the one who sits on the edge of the bed. Anna Wagner liked to keep a tidy house, so maybe she is the woman who likes to clank the dishes. A bigger mystery is the identity of the young girl who has been seen sitting on the box fan. Maybe the ghosts seen were none of these.

CHAPTER 12

HARDESTY MANSION

In the previous chapter, Absalom Karn's daughter Mary Malinda was mentioned. She married Francis Marion Hardesty, who co-owned the Hardesty Mill on High Street with his brother, William Kirk Hardesty. Their original mill was on Second Street Northwest just behind Karn's furniture store. The mill on Second Street was torn down, and materials from it were used to build the new mill on High Street adjacent to the Butler farm. These brothers were the grandsons of Reverend William Hardesty, who built the first gristmill in Malvern, Ohio. Reverend Hardesty also started the town of Malvern, which he named Troy. William Hardesty had served as a circuit-riding preacher for the Methodist Episcopal Church and was serving the little church in the area now known as Malvern. When he learned that a canal was going to come through that area, he purchased land and settled down. The land was purchased in 1816, and a log home was built to house the family. Then in 1824, William Hardesty built a brick home on the hill overlooking his gristmill and the town of Troy. It took three years to build the brick home.

In 1836, Reverend Hardesty's granddaughter Susanna died just two days shy of her first birthday. The family burial plot would begin with her burial. Located at the back of the property, this little cemetery is only accessible by foot. Nine years later, Reverend Hardesty's grandson and namesake, William Francis Hardesty, was buried near Susanna. William Francis was only four months old. A year later, Reverend Hardesty was buried with his grandchildren. Thirty-six gravestones have been located in

The Hardesty Mansion in the process of being restored. *Courtesy N8 Lane.*

this cemetery. Legend tells of other burials that are not marked by stones, and for good reason.

The legend states that Reverend Hardesty built his large home not only for his wife and twelve children but also to hide runaway slaves. Prior to the official title of Underground Railroad, Reverend Hardesty was helping folks leave their lives of slavery and make their way north, likely into Canada. On one occasion, William was transporting a couple from either Bolivar or Lisbon in a false-bottomed wagon, as he had done many times before. But this time, the couple he was transporting fell ill. He was unable to bring the couple back to health, and they passed away and were buried on the property. Because they were runaways, the family could not mark these graves.

A 1973 book on county cemeteries listed this little cemetery but claimed only six stones and said that two belonged to Confederate soldiers. While no records indicate that this is true, it does not mean they were not. The known soldiers in this cemetery are all said to have served on the Union side. Of the known graves, several were children, and the rest were either family or neighbors and likely attendees of Reverend Hardesty's church. A record from the 1970s indicated a girl named Justine was buried there on May 11, 1901, but there is nothing more than a handwritten note that

Reverend George Hardesty, son of William Hardesty, who founded what is now Malvern, Ohio. George died in the house and is buried in the family cemetery plot in the back. *Courtesy the Hardesty family from the Paul Hardesty collection and posted to FindaGrave.com by Jason Lombardi.*

says the stone was also chalked to get this information. The cemetery had become completely overgrown from neglect, and recently, local volunteers cleaned up this cemetery and found thirty-six graves.

In 1850, William's wife, Louisa, was buried beside him. The house then became the property of their son George, who was also a Methodist pastor. George and his wife, Hannah Hillerman, enlarged the home despite having no children of their own. George stayed plenty busy. He not only served as pastor for the nearby Methodist church but was also the first mayor of the newly formed Malvern. George served as the first banker and the postmaster from February 3, 1841, until January 28, 1848. When the school was formed, he served as a board member. Reverend George inherited not only his father's home but the gristmill as well. When George passed away in 1875, he, too, was buried in a plot in the family cemetery. His wife, Hannah, died in 1883 and was the last known burial in the little cemetery. Given the

The back of the Hardesty Mansion. *Courtesy N8 Lane.*

dates of William's and Louisa's deaths, it is more likely that George and Hannah were the ones operating the Underground Railroad stop.

So, what makes this house haunted? A group of paranormal investigators had the opportunity to spend the night before the home's most recent sale. One of the paranormal investigators referred to a hole in the basement as a "portal to hell." The hole is located in the addition made by George and Hannah. Due to a strong musty odor "like a swamp," one of the investigators refused to enter the basement and stayed upstairs while the others went down. While he was waiting, he saw a shadow form in the front doorway. The shadow slowly filled the space and then moved farther in. It moved across the room and then went up the stairs to the second floor. The investigator checked to see what could have been on the front porch creating this shadow and discovered that it was an enclosed porch with no exits or entrances other than the one into the house.

Meanwhile, in the basement, the others were checking the hole in the floor. One of the gentlemen had a pocketknife, which was pulled from his pocket and thrown across the basement floor by unseen hands. Then they heard banging upstairs, as if someone were smacking the doors with a sledgehammer. Quickly rejoining their friend on the first floor, they all witnessed a little girl walk across the railing on the stairs above them. The gentlemen calmed down and tried to re-create the things they had just witnessed but could not make the things happen—not even the shadow from the front door.

Still trying to figure out what they had witnessed in the house, they noticed an apparition in the backyard. Following it, they were led to the old family burial plot near the back of the seven-acre farm. The shadow vanished once they arrived at the cemetery.

Remember the hole in the basement floor? It is likely not a portal to hell. As mentioned earlier, one of the Hardesty men likely served as a conductor on the Underground Railroad. During the height of that operation, spies would watch houses they believed were involved in the aid of slaves who were escaping. One indicator was the amount of water used by a household. If it looked like the family was drawing more water than necessary for the known occupants, it was enough to search the home. Many homeowners took care of this by building additions on to their homes that covered the well. This way, they could draw water without being watched. The addition of this home that covers the well was built around 1863 during the height of the Underground Railroad. This knowledge seems to confirm the tale of the runaways who are possibly buried in the Hardesty Cemetery and is much more likely than a portal to hell.

So, who was the little girl the investigators saw upstairs? There are several graves belonging to young children but only one with a little girl older than an infant. Her name was Emma Sholl, and she was almost three when she died. Other than her gravestone, there seem to be no records of Emma. There is no record of her birth or death. Her parents, David and Mariah Sholl, moved with their three remaining children to Van Wert, Ohio, in 1864.

The shadow in the doorway could have been caused by the trees outside, or it could have been one of the former tenants who died in the house. Besides the three known Hardesty family members, there were at least three other known deaths. The next known death was Hope Marguerite Lewis, who died in the house in 1900, just eight days after the birth of her son Charles. Her husband, Joseph, later married Rose Randles Kirkpatrick, who was a widow. Together, they raised his two children and her three. After their deaths, Joseph's daughter Nadyne sold the house in 1943 to Leo Schafer, who converted it into apartments.

During the 1950s, two different tenants of the apartments died in the house. Both were older gentlemen, and they died within weeks of each other. The first was Samuel H. Hine. Hine; his wife, Alma; and their son Arletis were listed in the 1950 census in the Hardesty house. On April 20, 1951,

Hine's obituary appeared in the local papers and said he died of a cerebral hemorrhage. This could have been caused by many things but was most likely a stroke.

His next-door neighbor, who lived on the other side of the wall in the same house, was a gentleman by the name of Alonzo Guy Hewitt. Hewitt was also known as "Budgie." Budgie was found "dead in his bed" on June 2, 1951, but no cause of death was listed. Budgie died just a little over a month after Hine. Both men were in their seventies, but it seems odd they died so close together. If Hine died from an aneurysm or the hemorrhage was caused by high blood pressure, the sudden death may be keeping him in the house. Or Budgie might not have just simply passed in his sleep, as neighbors suspected.

With so many deaths in the house and a cemetery on the land, none of the living can know for certain who is haunting this house. It does seem peculiar to discover that not only does the home have a connection to the Karn house in Carrollton, but the census records from 1910 also show a connection to the Kintner family. Hiram Kintner was living next door with his mother, Keturah. Hiram's father was Andrew Kintner, a grandson of Christian and Maria Lamb Kintner, parents of Clement. Yet another haunted house with a Kintner connection.

CHAPTER 13
ATWOOD NURSING CENTER

My first thought when told I should investigate the "nursing home" was of the Golden Age Retreat. It made sense to me since it is a very old brick building. I had also learned that a few of the previous ghosts I researched had worked at or lived in the county infirmary that became the Golden Age Retreat. However, this was not the building or the location anyone was referring to. Nor was it the original county infirmary, which would have been in use in the 1850s. That county infirmary used to sit along what is now Alamo Road. It has long been gone, and out of respect to the recent passing of the land's owner, we will save it for another time. I did, however, go to the Golden Age Retreat and inquire of the current employees if they had ever experienced anything strange. After all, it was not all that long ago that coffins were discovered while digging for an expansion of Kensington Road.

The current employees all said, "No, but have you looked into the Atwood Nursing Center?" This was a home that had been closed for so long, I had forgotten it ever existed. I was immediately reminded of tales I had heard as a teenager. Classmates often talked about wanting to spend the night in the house, even though it was occupied. Tales of strange things happening in the house were told all the time. Of course, back then I had no idea I would someday be writing about ghosts, so I kept no record of those occurrences. But what could be creepier than an abandoned nursing home? Especially one that has sat empty for over twenty years. The former Atwood Nursing Center was barely visible behind the overgrowth of trees and bushes and seemed to have begged to be haunted.

The remains of the Atwood Nursing Center. *Janice Lane collection.*

The first stories shared were told by former employees who worked there only briefly. It seemed that no one ever worked there for very long. A former nurse told me she watched file folders be pulled out of a drawer and drop to the floor by invisible hands. Another said he saw shadows move from room to room. The most common report was of items moving by themselves, even large pieces of furniture. After one of the residents had passed, her furniture was divided among the living residents. A small sofa was moved to the day room. The next morning, all of the furniture had been placed back into her room, just as if she had never left. The staff accused each other of playing tricks. The pieces were again distributed among the residents. Again, the furniture returned to the deceased resident's room. The staff finally gave up and left the furniture in her room.

I spoke with ghost hunter Rick Weals, who owns Carroll County Paranormal Investigators LLC. He has given a few tours of the house over the years and said the things he saw there were not so much scary as intriguing. He called the house a hotbed of activity. Using a Kinect SLS camera designed for spotting ghosts, he captured at least one entity that he could confirm. The camera was set up in one of the old bedrooms. The leather chair and bed of the former occupant sat as they had when the home was in use. The camera was focused on the leather chair and indeed picked up movement, as if someone was sitting there. While Weals was trying to decide if it was an actual ghost sitting in the chair or just the camera picking up a reading from the leather, the figure stood up, walked across the room, and laid down on the bed. Weals was certain at that point he had just witnessed a ghost. A similar thing happened when a group of men from Hauntings of Ohio filmed the same room. Using an app on a laptop that worked very similarly to the Kinect camera, they also showed what looked like an extremely fidgety person sitting in the leather chair.

In this same room, Weals witnessed the figure stand and go to the closet. He described the entity as very tall, its head very near the door jam. After witnessing these things, he called a former nurse and asked if anyone really tall had lived at the home. She said yes, that would have been Leodis, and when she described the room Leodis used to live in, she confirmed that it was the same room they had all filmed. The only Leodis recorded as having lived in the house was Leodis Lampley, who was moved to a home in Akron, where he died in 2005. So, was it Leodis? Or something else?

Other experiences occurred in the former office. Hauntings of Ohio caught on tape, with the same computer program, a figure busily messing with files. One of Hauntings of Ohio's members said she had seen a shadowy figure in the corner of that room earlier in the evening. A distinctive red file folder moved from the desk to the floor, seemingly by itself, just like a former nurse had described. Weals also inquired of his nurse friend if anyone other than employees had been allowed in the office. She said no but then changed her mind when she remembered Mary Jane. Mary Jane Shultz was confined to a wheelchair but was sweet and helpful, so they would let her come in to the office to help. Mary Jane did have one flaw: she liked to goose people. Apparently, death has not stopped her from doing so! While setting up their equipment, Weals saw a figure sitting beside his friend. The friend startled and claimed he had been goosed. Mary Jane did not die in the house either, but the stories of her goosing people matches the scenario of what was happening. What would make these ghosts come back if they did not die there?

Some of the "residents" at the nursing home are friendly like Mary Jane. They like to do things like roll a ball across the floor in the day room. While touring the second floor of the building, the same lady who saw the shadow in the office felt someone tug on her hat, as if trying to get her attention. She also felt someone tap her shoulder when there was no one behind her. Other ghosts are a little scarier and have taken to doing things like crawling up the walls and across the ceiling in various rooms. One investigator entered a room and immediately felt a cold spot. At first, they all blamed a hole in the ceiling, but after he complained about something on his back, they saw there were fresh scratch marks. Yet there was no one behind him, and he had not run into anything.

Other than Leodis and Mary Jane, the names of the other ghosts have not been found. The home may have been closed for over twenty years, but it was in operation for at least forty. That is a lot of time for folks to have passed on there. It was first opened as the Carroll Pines and was operated by Thelma Jean Miller. By 1972, it had become the Royal Host Nursing Home and was operated by Earl and Anna Hershberger. Around 1985, it became the Atwood Nursing Center. The owner at that time was Robert Van Sickle, who also owned a nursing home in Mahoning County, Ohio. In September 2007, it was discovered that Van Sickle had taken out multiple loans against the properties and failed to report them to the state, nor had he paid back the banks. The employees and communities where these homes were located were unaware of this problem and were shocked when the residents were moved to other area homes and the building in Carrollton was abandoned.

Prior to becoming a nursing home, this was a quiet family farm. Members of the family were surprised to hear the reports of hauntings. Neighbors are also doubtful that the stories are true. One neighbor does believe and thinks the ghosts often venture out, as he has seen a few wandering around Guess Motors, which is on the same road.

While researching the property to learn of its past, it was discovered that it used to connect to the Bluebird Park Farm when it was owned by the Kintners. There is that name again. Stranger still was the other neighbor, Daniel Aller. Daniel was the son of John and Mary Christina Kintner Aller. As stated before, it is a small town, but it does seem intriguing that these two surnames keep surfacing in the research.

Unlike the other properties that need to be left alone, if you truly want to see this one for yourself, tours can be arranged by contacting Rick Weals through his Facebook page, Carroll County Paranormal Investigators LLC. If you are curious and do not want to go inside for yourself, you can go to YouTube and watch the episode recorded by Hauntings of Ohio. It is season two, episode five and is dated December 2020. Again, please reach out to these folks and do not go without permission. The current owners of the building are reasonable people but do not need trespassers who might get hurt. The house is in very poor condition.

CHAPTER 14
HELFRICH HOUSE

Have you checked the old apartments across from the funeral home?"

"What about the old Lincke apartments?"

"That big old building by the school has some stories."

Statements like this were made to me many times and referred to the same place. Reports from recent tenants sounded like all the other stories of haunted locations.

"I would hear footsteps when no one was around."

"Doors and cabinets open all by themselves."

"I saw strange shadows move across the room."

These are all things that could happen naturally when you live in an apartment building. Footsteps could be those of a neighbor simply coming home from work. The building is over one hundred years old, so movement in one part of the building could cause a door or cabinet door to swing open in another part. But what about the shadows? How would one explain those? Maybe the sun reflected off a passing car just right, and it created a shadow. Yet all of these instances seem to be extremely common in haunted places. Some can be explained by simple investigation, but others cannot.

A former tenant shared their experience while living in one of the apartments. They were so distraught over the experience they asked to remain anonymous and refused even to disclose which apartment they had lived in. It was early evening when the tenant arrived home. They could hear someone in the kitchen; cabinet doors were banging, dishes were rattling, and water was running—all noises as if someone were making dinner.

But the tenant lived alone. As the tenant neared the kitchen, all the noises stopped, and they entered just in time to see a shadow move across the room and disappear through a wall.

The tenant quickly packed a bag and went to a friend's house for the night. The next evening, the tenant went back to their own apartment, and this time, they did not hear any noises, but a shadowy figure was sitting at their dining table. Upon seeing the tenant, the figure once again scurried off through the wall of the kitchen. The tenant immediately moved out.

So, who was this shadowy figure so intent on making dinner? A search for the history of the building showed that it was built around 1846 by Adam Crozier. He bought the property from Jacob Shawke, who had purchased it from the town founder, Peter Bohart. Crozier had to purchase parts of two other lots to accommodate the large house. Soon after the house was finished, it was sold to Richard Runion. Almost immediately, Runion sold to James G. Wilson, who turned around and sold it to Jacob Helfrich, a name most longtime citizens of the county will remember.

Jacob Helfrich was born in Germany. When he turned eighteen, he boarded a ship bound for America. It took 105 days before they finally arrived in Baltimore, Maryland. From there, Jacob walked to Wheeling, Virginia (now West Virginia). He spent three months in Wheeling working at his trade of shoemaker. Using the money earned in those three months, Helfrich went by boat to Steubenville, Ohio. From Steubenville, he boarded a stagecoach with the intention of going to Crawford County, Ohio, where two of his brothers were already living. Along the way, the stagecoach got stuck in mud and was unable to proceed any farther. Helfrich found himself stuck in a little village called Carrollton. Liking the area, he opened a shoemaking business and thus remained in the little town.

Helfrich became a prominent figure in the little town of Carrollton. Not only did he have a thriving shoemaking business, but he also became a co-owner of the Carrollton and Oneida Railroad and served as a director of the railroad and general ticket agent. He also served as a justice of the peace.

He married Catherine Stemple in 1841, and they had nine children, which seems to be a good reason to live in such a large house. Jacob opened a shoemaking business in a front room on the first floor while the family resided in the rest of the building. Their son John went into the watch, clock, and jewelry trade and jointly occupied the space with his father for several years. John was very well known for his large clocks that once graced the sidewalks of Carrollton and was the one who installed the clock on the courthouse that is still used today.

This was the home of the Helfrich family. The shoe store was located where the woman and child are sitting in this photo, taken in the early 1920s or 1930s. *Courtesy John Davis.*

Catherine Helfrich was the first recorded death in the house. She died of old age on February 23, 1899, and her obituary sang her praises as a faithful churchgoer and all-around nice person. Nine years later, Jacob Helfrich also succumbed to old age and joined his beloved Catherine. Their daughter Susannah inherited the house. She had married Reverend Franklin Harsh, who served as a Lutheran pastor in Marion County, Ohio. When he died suddenly in 1869, Susannah moved back to Carrollton and lived in the Helfrich house with her parents. After the death of her father, a niece, Elta Frederick, moved in to help care for Susannah.

Susannah was known for her charity and ability to remember things. She was known to both her family and neighbors as Aunt Susie. Her obituary tells of a scrapbook that contained important history of the town and biographies of her family and friends. Facts were so fixed in her mind that moments before her death, she recalled, "Father died twenty-eight years ago today." Susannah Harsh was buried beside her father in Grandview Cemetery near her mother and four of her siblings. Two of her sisters are buried elsewhere in Ohio, and a baby brother was also buried in Grandview, but in a different part of the cemetery.

Since Susannah had no children of her own, she left the house to her niece Elta Frederick. Elta lived in the house all alone for the next ten years. She never married and, perhaps out of loneliness, moved back to Butler, Pennsylvania. In 1946, she sold the house to her neighbor, Dr. Carl Lincke. Dr. Lincke's office sat behind the Helfrich house, and he converted the home into apartments.

Everything about the Helfrich family seems sweet and innocent and shows no cause as to why someone in the family would be haunting their home. That is, until I began looking closely at the deaths of the nine children. Most of the family is buried in section B of Grandview Cemetery, but two stones are in section I. One stone is that of Albert, who died when he was a year old. Next to him is the stone of Mary E. It was chalked by someone and posted to Findagrave.com. This stone says Mary Elizabeth was born on October 8, 1852, and died at the age of twelve on April 23, 1865. This is odd because all other records show Mary Elizabeth living to adulthood and marrying J. Henry Troutman. A marriage license dated September 15, 1881, was found in the Carroll County marriage records, and she is listed as Mrs. J. Henry Troutman in the Beers Biographical Sketch from 1891. A newspaper article in the *Carroll Free Press* dated April 15, 1891, lists "J.H. Troutman, wife and three children" as attending a wedding anniversary party for Mr.

The Helfrich house as it looks in 2024. *Janice Lane collection.*

and Mrs. Jacob Helfrich. Mary Elizabeth is also listed in both the 1860 and 1870 census records. So, who died in 1865? Why is there a stone for Mary Elizabeth if she did not die? If the stone was for a different Mary Elizabeth, then why is the birthdate the same? Why are the parents the same? The stone says, "Daughter of J&C Helfrich," yet there are no records indicating the birth of two children with the same name being born to this couple.

While this is quite mysterious, it still does not seem to connect with the strange occurrences in the old family homestead. There seems to be no logical explanation as to who was making all that noise in the former tenant's kitchen. Again, as it has been turned into apartments, it is not likely to find other deaths that occurred in the house.

CHAPTER 15

CONCLUSION

While this is the end of this book, it is certainly not the end of the stories. The research of each place included here has left me with more questions than answers. Perhaps you, too, lost count of just how many times the same families seemed to come up. Do the family connections have something to do with why they are all still hanging around? It is also interesting to note that every single building is made of brick. Do bricks have something to do with it? They seem to hold a special connection at the Cox Mansion. One of the paranormal investigators thought perhaps bricks hold more energy since they often came from the land the house was built on. Maybe. The Voodoo religion believes bricks hold energy that will protect you. Perhaps we have another question that we will likely never find an answer to. And just what happened to the ghosts whose buildings were torn down? Again, we will likely never know.

My family thought I should include the things that happened to me as I investigated and wrote this book. Some were witnessed by others, some were not. As I began planning the book, I was desperately searching for some old compact discs of photos that I had not seen in years. I was about to give up when my husband and I both heard a noise on the front porch, like the mail being delivered. It was much earlier in the day than normal for a mail delivery, but I went to the porch to see. It is an enclosed porch, and the mailbox sits just outside. There was nothing in the mailbox. I turned to go back into the main part of the house when a box I thought our daughter had brought home from college fell over slightly. I went to put it back and decided to look inside. There, nestled safely in a basket, were all forty-three discs!

Not strange enough for you? I was at the Genealogical Society Library looking for obituaries. The one I wanted to read was listed in the index but was not in its supposed location. The ladies helping me that day also looked, to no avail. We moved on to look for other information on the family, and I was looking through a three-ring binder filled with old photos when a small slip of paper fell out. I picked it up, and it was the missing obituary. The ladies just shook their heads, not sure what to believe.

Some of my "ghosts" are not as helpful. As I sat trying to type this, my computer screen randomly went black. Try as I might, nothing was allowing it to come back on. I could hear it humming, I could see a faint light that indicated it had not died, but nothing. I walked away for a few minutes, and when I came back, there was still nothing. Needless to say, I was near tears, since I was so close to completion of this manuscript. Taking a deep breath, I said a quick prayer and then noticed a candle my bestie had given me as a souvenir from Louisiana. It says it's to keep a house safe. I do not believe in such power but said another prayer, lit the candle, and waved it around the computer, and the screen suddenly came back. A thank you to God, and I was back in business. Although I did lose the web pages I had been reading, it was easy enough to find them again.

I was picking up the final proofreading from my friend DiAnne when the last strange occurrence happened. She was sharing with me some photos she had taken of a Ouija board that belonged to her grandmother. We had texted and called each other several times prior to that day. She selected the photos, chose my name from her contacts list, and hit send. I waited. After a few minutes, when her text did not deliver to me, we checked her phone. Two of the numbers had been transposed. She corrected the problem and saved the change. Once again, she tried to text me the photos. Still nothing. We went back to her contact list, and the numbers had transposed again! This time I sent a text from my phone to her, and as it arrived on her phone, we saw the previous wrong number vanish from her phone and the pictures suddenly sent to me. She laughed and said she was glad I had been standing there to witness this strange occurrence.

Still not sure if you believe or not? That's okay. Me neither. I truly do hope you've enjoyed reading these encounters, and I ask that you respect the privacy of others and leave ghosts and the living be. I know I have said it several times throughout this work, but do not go knocking on doors and asking for a séance or a ghost tour. Let the living, seen and unseen, be. Remember, we do not condone trespassing on any private property. Always seek permission before entering private property. The same goes for businesses. Feel free to visit the Virginia and enjoy a meal or a beer, but let the ghosts be. I hope reading of these encounters is enough.

One last thing. I have always been told that you do not begin writing with an apology, so I have saved that until the very end. To all of you whose story did not get told this time, I am so sorry. Perhaps there will be a volume two someday. Until then, enjoy!

BIBLIOGRAPHY

BeeKeepers Magazine 8, no. 1 (January 1881): 289.

Beers, J.H. *Commemorative Biographical Record of the Counties of Harrison and Carroll, Ohio*. N.p., 1891, 789.

Burwell, Adam. "The Passing Parade Beginning in 1873 As I Remember," *Carroll County Newsletter*, n.d.

Carroll County Park District. "History of Blue Bird Farm." ccparkdistrict. org/bluebirdfarmpark.html.

Carroll Free Press. "Confession of a Medium." April 23, 1852.

———. Letter to the Editor. March 26, 1852.

———. "The 'Spirit Rappings' in the Churches." April 22, 1853.

———. "Spiritual Rapping." December 24, 1852.

———. "Very Rich." May 5, 1853.

Carroll Journal. "Flames Rip Legendary Cox Mansion Saturday." 1969.

Daily Times (New Philadelphia, OH). March 3, 1881–April 21, 1881.

———. "No Clues Found in Ross Murder." September 3, 1925.

Detroit Urbex. Detroiturbex.com.

Find a Grave. FindAGrave.com.

Free Press Standard. "Peter Ross Brutally Slain by Unknown." September 3, 1925.

Griffin, Velma. "The Cox Mansion." *Free Press Standard*, 1978.

———. "Is Morges Rectory Haunted?" *Dover Times Reporter*, July 13, 1973.

Historic Map Works. HistoricMapWorks.com.

McCauley, Russell. "Ghostly Legends Lurk at Carroll County Site." *Canton Repository*, n.d.

Meyers, David, and Elise Meyers Walker. *Ohio's Black Hand Syndicate: The Birth of Organized Crime in America*. Charleston, SC: The History Press, 2018.

Moore, R. Laurence. "Spiritualism and Science: Reflections on the First Decade of the Spirit Rappings." *American Quarterly* 24, no. 4 (October 1972): 474–500.

Wege, Mairy Jayn. "Carroll Priest Used Exorcism at Rectory." *Plain Dealer* (Cleveland, OH), n.d.

Winkowski, Mary Ann. *When Ghosts Speak: Understanding the World of Earthbound Spirits*. New York: Grand Central Publishing, 2007.

About the Author

This is the fourth work Janice VanHorne-Lane has published with Arcadia Publishing and The History Press. Her other works include *Carroll County: A Place to Call Home, Carrollton: Then & Now* and *Safe Houses and the Underground Railroad in East Central Ohio*. Janice; her husband, Nathan; and their two daughters, Bailey and Emma, call Carrollton home. Janice has lived in Carroll County most of her life. When she isn't writing, Janice works as a secretary for Mt. Pleasant Methodist Church and can often be found at her storefront, Kase-n-Lane Eclectic Artisans, where she makes and sells custom handmade items. As a family, they enjoy traveling to do research for her history books, as well as attending craft shows.

FREE eBOOK OFFER

Scan the QR code below, enter your e-mail address and get our original Haunted America compilation eBook delivered straight to your inbox for free.

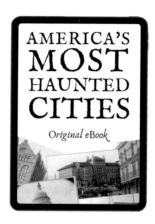

ABOUT THE BOOK

Every city, town, parish, community and school has their own paranormal history. Whether they are spirits caught in the Bardo, ancestors checking on their descendants, restless souls sending a message or simply spectral troublemakers, ghosts have been part of the human tradition from the beginning of time.

In this book, we feature a collection of stories from five of America's most haunted cities: Baltimore, Chicago, Galveston, New Orleans and Washington, D.C.

SCAN TO GET
AMERICA'S MOST HAUNTED CITIES

Having trouble scanning? Go to:
biz.arcadiapublishing.com/americas-most-haunted-cities